RELATIONAL YOUTHWORK

YOUTH MINISTRY BOOKS

Relational Youthwork

Edited by Pete Ward

Published by Lynx Communications
Sandy Lane West, Oxford OX4 5HG
England
ISBN 0 7459 3223 1

Albatross Books Pty Ltd
PO Box 320, Sutherland
NSW 2232, Australia
ISBN 0 7324 1247 1

First edition 1995
All rights reserved
Printed and bound in Great Britain

ACKNOWLEDGMENTS

Scripture quotations taken from the Holy
Bible, New International Version. Copyright
© 1973, 1978, 1984 by International Bible
Society. Used by permission of Hodder &
Stoughton Ltd, a member of the Hodder
Headline Group.

Illustrations by Matthew Buckley

CONTENTS

LIST OF CONTRIBUTORS

Sam Adams is Director of Oxford Youthworks.

Peter Ball is National Youth Officer of the Church of England.

Christine Cook is Director of Contact-Jeunes, Switzerland.

Bob Mayo is Chaplain to South Bank University.

Mark H. Senter III is Professor of Youth Ministry at Trinity Evangelical Seminary, Chicago, United States.

Steve Tilley is Head of The Church Youth Fellowships Association.

Pete Ward is The Archbishop of Canterbury's Advisor for Youth Ministry, Tutor in Theology and Oxford Youthworks, and Honorary Research Fellow at the Centre for Theology and Education, Trinity College, Carmarthen.

FOREWORD

As we approach the end of this century, it is more important than ever that the church takes young people and youth culture seriously. I have often quoted the saying that 'the church is only ever one generation away from extinction', but the need for young people to be playing an active part in the life of the church is about much more than mere survival or numerical growth.

Historically, both in the church and outside it, young people have acted as agents of change. Their enthusiasm, freshness and vitality have often been the spur to spiritual renewal. At times, sadly, that enthusiasm has been dampened by others either through a refusal to change or from a fear of change. It is these issues, amongst others, that must be addressed if young people are to be enabled to play a proper role in the life of the church.

But change in the church should never be reckless or ill-considered. It needs to be backed by reflection, prayer and careful thought. For this reason, amongst others, I am delighted to commend the Lynx Youth Ministry Books as a useful tool to enable people to assess the process of change.

It is sad that we have sometimes thought of youth ministry as something which anyone can do without requiring any training or testing of their aptitude for the task. The demands now being made by the Children Act amongst other things are forcing us to look afresh at the particular skills needed by those caring for young people. In this context we should not ignore the many insights to be found in secular youthwork courses—nor should we be bound by them.

Christian youth ministry has its own characteristics. It is different from secular youth ministry. Whilst it is true that many of the core values of good Christian youthwork are by no means unique or particularly innovative, the timeless gospel of Christ needs to be proclaimed and incarnated afresh in every age and culture. In other words, it is itself subject to change.

Three particular areas stand out for me as ones that need to be urgently addressed:

The Bible: No one knows the full extent of the changes being brought about by the information technology revolution. More words are being produced than ever before—as are more video images—but the hunger I have seen for the Bible in many parts of the globe stands in stark contrast to the lack of enthusiasm for it in many parts of the Western world. The picture is made more complex still by the fact that many are no longer asking 'truth' questions. 'Does it work?' and 'How does it feel?' have often replaced the question 'Is it true?' Yet the latter is a question the Bible is constantly raising and is one we have to face for ourselves. Every youth minister needs to find ways of bringing this to young people within the context of their own culture. This is a daunting, but exhilarating, challenge and one which can be enormously rewarding when the Bible comes alive to a generation who often know little or nothing about it.

Worship: When I visited Taizé young people would often contrast the simplicity of the worship they experienced there with church services back at home. There was a simplicity about the worship of the brothers which spoke deeply to many of the 1,000 young people I travelled with. Yet part of the charm and power of the Taizé style of worship is the richness of the Christian tradition represented in their worship. The way that they use traditional words from the psalms and Christian liturgy, the use of icons and signs such as making a cross. For some of the young people from an evangelical tradition these ways of worship were new and strange, but many expressed their appreciation of them. Taizé in these ways points us to the truth that in looking for new forms of worship the Christian tradition is a rich, exciting resource.

Relationship: Community and fellowship are central to church life. Many young people are searching for a sense of identity and personhood. It is in relationship, firstly with God but also with each other, that we find ourselves to be who we are. If the church is to welcome young people then we need to find ways to build and foster relationships between adults and young people, because these relationships are the threads which bind the whole together. When I was in Durham each summer members of the church would invite non-Christian people to go away on a sailing and canoeing holiday we called Watersports. In a relaxed atmosphere, through having fun together, we were able to share the Christian faith. Watersports was able to cross not only faith barriers but also generational ones as teenagers and older people within the church shared in Christian mission together. Now, I realize that an idea such as Watersports is not for everyone, yet in its emphasis upon relationships and friendship outreach surely it expresses a deep, enduring aspect of the gospel? Relationships are the context within which people find God and in doing so they also find themselves and each other. Relationships and the gospel, therefore, go hand in hand.

The church needs to find relevant and sustainable ways of building relationships with those young people who at present are socially and culturally excluded from the church. To do this we need committed people who have heard God's call to give themselves in relationship to young people.

These are some of the key areas youth ministers need to reflect on and it is my hope that this series will help to inspire a generation of such people to reach out in the name of Christ to young people.

ARCHBISHOP OF CANTERBURY

PREFACE

Christians have been involved in working with young people from the days that youthwork was invented. We have a long history of action, but we have been less impressive in developing a well-articulated and theologically informed body of knowledge. Most literature on Christian youthwork has been designed to provide quick solutions at an easy-to-use 'how to do it' level. Doing youthwork has always got to be primary, but the lack of any serious consideration of practice could be a fatal long-term weakness.

The Lynx Youth Ministry Books aim to provide a forum where the theory of youth ministry can be discussed. The first two volumes, *Relational Youthwork* and *The Church and Youth Ministry*, present a series of articles specially written for the series. The intention has been to gather a diversity of views in a single volume to foster further discussion and debate rather than to set down the definitive word on any subject. The authors discuss Christian work amongst young people from a variety of perspectives. Their views are, of course, their own, rather than those of the editor or of Lynx Communications.

The volumes are designed for use in the training of youthworkers and clergy as well as being accessible for those who wish to keep informed as to developments within youth ministry. The material is presented at a basic academic level. A number of the papers in these volumes were presented at the Conference for Youth Ministry held at Mansfield College, Oxford in January 1995.

PETE WARD, OXFORD 1995

1

Christian relational care

PETE WARD

Introduction

For the past ten years I have been involved in a Christian youthwork project called Oxford Youthworks. Oxford Youthworks is a training centre running courses in Christian youthwork, but more importantly it is an alliance of like-minded people. This alliance has grown up around the way that we as a group of Christian adults choose to involve ourselves in the lives of young people. Our alliance has not been based on similarities in Christian doctrine, nor on our affection for each other, neither is it a function of working together for one organization. Our alliance has sprung from the way that we feel compelled to do youthwork.

This chapter is an attempt to express in theoretical terms the way that we do youthwork.[1] Ten years is a long time for any youthwork project to be running. Now seems an appropriate moment to attempt to make theoretical sense of the way we engage in the lives of young people. In the first instance, this attempt to create theory from practice is for our own self-understanding. It is my hope that youthworkers within Oxford Youthworks and those associated with us will see the pattern of their work amongst young people reflected in this chapter. Whilst some of the words I use will be unfamiliar, this is because I am self-consciously attempting to create an appropriate terminology for our work. It is my hope that this chapter will be recognized as an expression of our unity in practice.

Over the past ten years those within Oxford Youthworks have tended to use a number of different phrases to describe our youthwork. All of these have to some extent or another been open to misunderstanding. One reason for this is that terms such as 'contact', 'relational youthwork' and 'incarnational youthwork' generally only describe a part of what we do. To define our work we need to create a phrase which expresses our practice in its entirety. My suggestion is 'Christian relational care'.

Deciding on an appropriate term for our work is, I realize, only half of the problem. 'Christian relational care' is an empty phrase justifiably accused of being jargon. I am not, however, apologetic about this fact since I am firmly of the belief that theory is a construct which relies for its validity on the practice on which it is based. I use the term 'Christian relational care' in the full realization that it is artificial. The extent to which it adequately represents and serves practice will, I realize, be its true value. What will give this term mileage will be its ability to express the way in which the people who make up Oxford Youthworks are involved on a day-to-day basis in the lives of young people.

Christian relational care: 'Christian'

Central to the work of Oxford Youthworks is a sense of vocation. This vocation arises from the Christian commitment of each of the youthworkers. All of the staff would agree, even if we did not generally use the term, that God has in some way 'called' us to work with young people. Every youthworker can point to a time or a process or an experience that has led them to believe that God was inviting them to be 'youth ministers'.

Vocation is crucial to the operation of Christian relational care. In the first place, as youthworkers we know that our relationships with young people can be extremely demanding. Caring for needy young people can be very stressful. Most of us have from time to time asked ourselves why we are doing this kind of work. In these circumstances what keeps us going is our conviction that God has asked us to be involved in the lives of young people. Secondly, we all realize that our ministry is sustained by our spiritual lives. None of us would continue in this work without a regular encounter with God in prayer and worship. This may simply be asking for guidance, 'God what should I do next?', but more often it is through the contemplation of Christ in the scriptures that we are inspired to renewed effort in our work with young people.

Vocation is also about our own sense of who we are. The belief that we are invited by God to be engaging in the lives of young people is core to the practice of Christian relational care. Each of us would see our faith as central to who we are as people. Our faith is an integrating factor which pervades everything that we do. To engage in a relationship with a young person therefore means that we bring everything we are to that encounter. In this way we are fully aware that faith and being are essential to our practice of youthwork. Young people regularly ask us about ourselves, indeed this kind of mutual sharing is right at the heart of the relationships which we are attempting to build. The 'Christianness' of what we are doing inevitably comes out in these conversations.

Given that vocation and faith are the starting-point for expressing the ideas behind Oxford Youthworks, it is clear that I should start by exploring how our sense of vocation is inspired by theological reflection and prayer. This vocation is Christian because we are convinced that it is rooted in Christ. To say this is to draw upon traditions of spiritual life and vitality which have consistently inspired us and challenged us to renewed effort. These traditions are to be found in biblical stories, pictures and theological themes which we hold in common at Oxford Youthworks. Our practice as youthworkers is intimately connected to this tradition.

THE MISSION OF GOD

We recognize that our sense of call is intrinsically linked to the mission of God in the world. Bosch defines God's mission as:

God's self revelation as the One who loves the world, God's involvement in and with the world, the nature and activity of God, which embraces both the Church and the world, and in which the Church is privileged to participate. Missio Dei enunciates the good news that God is God-for-people.[2]

Our vocation arises from our conviction that God invites us as Christian people to share in his relational care for the world. We build relationships with young people because we are Christians. Indeed I would say that it is when we are following our call to build relationships with young people that we are being most Christian. It is perhaps too shallow to talk of our faith motivating us to do youthwork, because we feel this impulse to care for young people much more deeply than that. We care for young people because of who we are, that is people called by God to share in his mission.

THE INCARNATION AS PATTERN AND EXAMPLE

It is meditation and reflection on the manner of Christ's incarnation which has continued to inspire our involvement in the lives of young people. By incarnation I need to stress that this includes the whole gospel story, that is Jesus who was born, lived a life, died, rose again and reigns on high.

When Jesus prays for his disciples in John 17 he says, 'I sent them into the world, just as you sent me into the world.' John Stott makes the point that the emphasis of this verse is on the 'style' of our ministry.[3] The sense that there is a parallel between our own activity as youth ministers and the life of Christ has been a constant source of inspiration for Oxford Youthworks. To be engaged in a ministry of Christian relational care is in some sense to seek to imitate Christ. As we have studied the life of Christ and prayed through our practice as youth ministers, there have been recurring themes which have crucially affected the way we relate to young people.

⊙ The incarnation is the means of God's expression of care for the world. When John records that, 'The Word became a human being and, full of grace and truth, lived amongst us' (John 1:14), we have seen the way that God has chosen to reveal himself to humanity. This revelation was thoroughly relational. Theological debate about the incarnation has perhaps centred on the union of divine and human in Christ, yet it has been the force of the fact that God chose to live 'amongst us' that has continued to challenge and inspire Oxford Youthworks to do youth ministry. To be part of the mission of God and thus to seek to imitate Christ means that we must remain focused on relationships as a means of self-communication.

⊙ There is a particularity about the incarnation which places Jesus firmly in a historical and a cultural context. The political, economic and social context of the gospel narratives are by no means incidental to the ministry of Jesus. What is impressive in the Gospels is how Jesus seeks to make known the kingdom of God within this cultural world. The gospel, in this sense, is contextualized by the life of Christ. As we seek to imitate Christ as youth ministers, we also need to look for ways in which the gospel might be contextualized within youth culture. To do this we must first learn to understand and respect the cultural world of the young people with whom we are in relationship.

⊙ Philippians 2:5–8 makes it clear that the essence of incarnation was a self-emptying on the part of Christ: 'of his own free will he gave up all he had and took the nature of a servant' (verse 7). It is of the essence of Christian relational care that the youth minister lays aside any notion of 'professional status', 'expert training' or 'religious superiority'. Crucial to this process has been the belief that relationships with young people should be first established in places and social settings where the young people themselves feel comfortable and would normally gather. This might be the school playground or the streets, or whilst the young people are engaged in an activity they have freely chosen to adopt. This is in contrast to other youthwork which has tended to be focused on areas where the youthworker is in control, for example youth club or church meeting.

Self-emptying, however, also needs to cover the social agenda of the youth minister. The church in England has been rightly criticized for attempting to use youthwork, especially amongst working-class young people, as a form of social control.[4] A good deal of Christian youthwork has tended to be driven by the concerns and moral panics of the middle classes.[5] Funding for church work has often followed such anxieties. Christian relational care in contrast attempts to work with young people on the concerns which they themselves wish to address. The youth minister imitates Christ in becoming a 'servant'. The kingdom of God emerges from the relationship between the youth minister and young people as a dynamic process inspired by God's activity in the lives of young people, rather than from the agenda of an authoritarian, middle-class church. In adopting these roles, we are consciously learning from traditions of theological reflection and engagement in community life, which have been worked out in marginalized communities primarily in the Two Thirds World.[6]

⊙ Imitating Christ involves the youth minister in a life of self-sacrifice and service:

For even the Son of Man did not come to be served; he came to serve and to give his life to redeem many.
MARK 10:45

To imitate Christ is to follow the way of the cross. Relationships with young people are generally a great joy and source of encouragement, but every youth minister will, from time to time, be involved in tough, stressful relationships with hurting and battered young people. Real relationships involve commitment and cost. The spirituality and sense of call of each Christian youth minister is a vital source of strength in such situations.

THE SPIRITUALITY OF THE YOUTH MINISTER

Christian relational care is Christian because it is rooted in a disciplined spiritual encounter with Christ. Alongside the sense of call and vocation is the promise of Christ to his disciples to be with them (Matthew 28:20). It is our experience as youth ministers that our practice is enriched, encouraged and sustained by regular prayer and worship. It is in prayer that we experience the promise of Christ to be with us. As we pray we understand more clearly how our concerns for young people are also the concerns of God. In prayer we can bring the suffering that we encounter in the lives of young people to Christ who also suffered. In short, prayer not only keeps us going as youth ministers, it also transforms the relationships we have formed with young people, by recognizing their spiritual significance. God cares about them.

To pray for young people is an expression of the belief that Christian youthwork sees God as active in the world. Change, reconciliation, forgiveness and growth are as much spiritual realities as they are human. When we pray, or when we ask others to pray, for our work we are recognizing this fact. Christian relational care endorses the view that God is a vital source of energy and motivation not just for youthworkers, but also for young people.

Similarly worship, either in a church context or when we meet as a team, is an energizing and cleansing experience. It is in worship that we are able to lift the weight of the suffering of young people and celebrate the joys of their movement towards new life. Worship makes us whole. In worship we encounter God and we recognize our humanity. But worship also turns us towards young people and the communities of which we are a part. The closing prayer of the Anglican Communion Service makes this very clear when it says:

Almighty God,
We thank you for feeding us
with the body and blood of your Son, Jesus Christ.
Through him we offer you our souls and bodies to
be a living sacrifice.
Send us out in the power of your Spirit
to live and work
to your praise and glory. Amen.[7]

YOUNG PEOPLE ARE SPIRITUAL

Modernity tended to polarize Christian youthwork into church-based 'spiritual' activity and secular professional youthwork.[8] In recent years a debate concerning 'spiritual development' has been taking place within the youth service, but as yet it is unclear how a clear Christian commitment, which sees spiritual experience as essentially linked to Christ, might link with ideas of spiritual development. In effect spiritual development, for all its promise, leaves the Christian youth minister with much the same polarization as previously existed.

Christian relational care is concerned to challenge this polarization as reductive, not just of the Christian gospel, but also of the young people themselves. It has been our intention at Oxford Youthworks, through committed relationships, to demonstrate to young people that God shares their concerns, be they concerns for their future, for their community, for injustice, for their marginalization, for the breakup of their families, for their lack of an economic future, for their experience of discrimination and prejudice, or whatever. In equal measure, it should be stressed that God particularly delights in young people; in their care for each other, in their creativity, in their construction of identity through youth culture, in their activism in political and environmental issues, and in their excitement about their lives. In this context the role of the youth minister is to make concrete, by personal relationship and involvement, the spiritual reality of God's interest and engagement in these areas of young people's lives. Such engagement is Good News.

With this as a basis, young people may then begin to experience a God who comes alongside them in their world. Sharing the gospel in a verbal form then becomes simply the explanation of a reality that the young people have already, to some extent, experienced. Some may well decide to respond to a God who cares for them in such immediate ways. The task of youth ministry is to work with these young people to express a form of worship and prayer which fits their culture and their experience of God on a day-to-day basis as he engages with their lives.

Christian relational care: 'relational'

Christian relational care is not unique in stressing relationships as the basis for youthwork; indeed, it could be said that all youthwork has a relational base. This being the case, an explanation of Christian relational care needs to focus on the manner of the relationships built between the youth ministers and the young people. This focus upon relationships in youthwork finds its reference point in the Christian understanding of God who is trinity.

THE TRINITY AND RELATIONAL CARE

Trinitarian theology has traditionally seen God as Father, Son and Holy Spirit in a dynamic, caring relationship. Jesus' continual reference to his Father throughout the gospel tradition points to the intimacy of the trinity. The relationship of the trinity is however most sharply brought into focus in the co-operative expression of God's care for humanity seen in the life and the death of Christ.

I am the good shepherd. As the Father knows me and I know the Father, in the same way I know my sheep and they know me. And I am willing to die for them.
JOHN 10:14–15

The force of the gospel, that is the life, death, raising to life and reigning on high of Jesus is to invite humans into an intimate relationship with the divine. The effect of sharing in the atmosphere of trinitarian relational care is twofold. Firstly, disciples of Christ are to be bound together by love.

My commandment is this: love one another, just as I love you.
JOHN 15:12

The relational care of the trinitarian God is reflected in the care that disciples are to have for each other. This care, however, is not simply self-serving. Its expression, secondly, is to result in others coming to faith.

I pray not only for them, but also for those who believe in me because of their message. I pray that they may all be one, Father. May they be in us, just as you are in me and I am in you. May they be one so that the world will believe you sent me.
JOHN 17:20–21

It is the trinitarian nature of the God who has called us to care for young people which inspires us to act relationally in the way we minister. Relationships and love, which characterize the message of Christ to the disciples, however, also form the context and the method of relational care.

PERSONAL

When youthwork becomes 'professional', young people tend to become 'client groups' or 'cases'. In Christian relational care a high priority is placed on the personal in relationships. Christian youth ministry is not a job, it is a calling. The sense of vocation and personal involvement in building relationships means that young people are treated essentially as friends, not cases or clients. The youth ministers are involved in the local community and in the lives of young people for reasons which arise from the core of who they are, that is their faith commitment. In this sense Christian relational care rests on personal rather than professional relationships.

BOUNDARIES

Whilst stressing the personal nature of the relationships formed with young people, it is also central to Christian relational care that relationships between young people and adults need clear and well-understood boundaries if they are to remain healthy. At the root of these boundaries is the recognition that relational care places the needs of the young person before those of the adult youthworker. Where the needs of the youthworker begin to dictate the shape and direction of relationships problems begin to emerge.

Personal boundaries are also essential to maintain a healthy ministry amongst young people. Adult youthworkers should be sufficiently self-aware to recognize their own needs, for example for privacy, friendship, intimacy, status or sexual fulfilment. These needs are common to our humanity; however, they should be fulfilled outside of the practice of Christian relational care. To care for others, it is necessary to first care for oneself.[9]

Alongside personal boundaries there are also organizational values and perspectives which need to be maintained if we are to continue to work together in good relationship with each other and with the local community. These values within Oxford Youthworks include a commitment to: regular supervision, a shared code of morality, confidentiality within the team, and to a historic and orthodox expression of the faith.

WE'RE HERE BECAUSE...

The Christian youth minister is involved in the life of the local community, because he or she feels that God has asked them to 'be there'. Being there is the first and most crucial element of the expression of Christian relational care. Being there can take many forms. It could be that we work out with a group of weightlifters on a weekly basis. It could be that we support the local basketball team. It could be that we just sit with a group every lunchtime and check out the lads as they walk past. Being there is thoroughly relational because we are spending time with young people.

SPENDING TIME

Time is an expression of care. If you care for me then I expect you to 'spend time with me'. If you don't make space for me in your busy diary then I know that you don't really care. With Christian relational care this principle is made the focus of our life amongst young people. Our youth ministry has been built around regular social contact. Young people do not have to 'come to see us', we go to meet them in places where they ordinarily and regularly gather. So they need not make an appointment with us because they know that we will show up on their patch in a day or so.

AGENDA

The primary concern of the youth minister is 'being there' with young people and building friendships through informal social contact. In the normal course of things, issues such as racism, sexism, crime, drugs, truancy, family stress, and so on are regularly raised by young people. As an available adult friend, the youth minister may become a resource for the group. The youth minister may also feel that a particular situation calls for particular intervention on their behalf. From the perspective of funding agencies, schools or other professional bodies, it may well be that these specific activities are seen as the primary focus for regard and respect of the youth minister. This being the case, it should be said that these activities are well able to be measured as 'outcomes' of the work. However, such measurement is generally felt by the youth minister as to be somewhat reductive because the root of his or her work is relationship and 'being there'. Projects and activities are the result of committed time spent with groups of young people.

From the perspective of young people, particularly those who have regularly been involved with secular agencies, such activities and projects are perceived as being qualitatively different, because they are suggested by the youth minister who hangs out with them and has built trust over a period of years.[10] With many young people who are perceived as being at risk, our experience is that the relational approach by the youth minister has been the difference between the young person engaging in a particular project or not. Young people who have been previously seen as being outside of truancy or crime-related projects have made marked progress as a result of the work of a youth minister operating Christian relational care.

RELATIONSHIPS GROW

Contact between the youth minister and the young people will grow over a period of time. 'Being there' is a vital and necessary building block to the expression of care, and as such, it remains the mainstay of activity for the youth minister. Having said this, relationships will move on and more in-depth activity will begin to evolve. This will generally mean that activities are undertaken which take the youth minister and the young people beyond the context in which they normally meet. Activities could include going shopping, or visiting a rave or a rock concert together, or a visit to a young person's or to the youth minister's home. These contacts will continue to be friendship focused. Sometimes an activity will be suggested by the group of young people; at other times, the youth minister may wish to take the initiative. It is into this context that activities recognized by 'professional youthworkers' or by the Christian church may be set.

In the course of building relationships, a group of young people may begin to discuss particular issues, for example drugs, racism, unemployment. The youth minister, given the interest of the group, might suggest the idea of an informal get-together to look at this particular issue. For the youth minister, and for the young people, a discussion about drugs or any other subject is simply a development of their relationship. In this sense, this event may be little different in style or nature than a video night round at someone's house. The difference is that the youth minister is beginning to work with the issues raised by the young people and is acting as a resource person to the group.

It is common with professional youthwork and in relation to funding applications to dress up such group work as a 'project'. This language is also seen as reductive of the relational heart of Christian relational care since it tends to focus attention on group work as the main outcome of youthwork. Christian relational care will always tend to value relationships above projects.

RELATIONSHIPS AS A CONTEXT FOR CARE

A trinitarian theology of relational care points to the importance of the informal network of friendships and relationships which surround the youth minister who is in relationship with young people. Through sharing in activities and visits to the youthworker's home, place of work, or church-related events the young people are included in a network of caring relationships with a number of different Christian people. A young person, through these contacts, may begin to form friendships with a whole range of people who can provide an informal network of community care. One example could be a young person meeting a Christian through a shared friendship with the youth minister who has an interest in fishing or sport or music. Alongside the regular contact with the youthworker, other activities may then begin take place based on these interests.

Young people are often drawn into relationships with the relatives and family of the youth minister. Once again these contacts can offer a shared context of care and support for the young person. Such meetings and relationships also enrich the lives of the youth minister and their families and friends.[11]

Similarly, through a friendship with a young person, the youth minister may begin to build relationships with contacts in the young person's family and neighbourhood. It is not uncommon for a youth minister to become a source of friendship and support for parents and for whole families in times of crisis.

RELATIONSHIP WITH GOD

The premise of Christian relational care is that God wishes to be in relationship with young people. This perspective affirms the spiritual dimension to be integral to every aspect of the youth minister's practice. The youth minister is called to be involved with young people as an expression of God's desire to be in relationship with young people. In this sense, the practice of Christian relational care is the concrete, day-to-day, living out of God's commitment to young people. In this context, speaking about 'the gospel' becomes an understandable explanation of God's invitation to relationship expressed in the relational care of the youth minister. Some young people may actively take up this invitation to relationship, that is, to be in relationship with God as a Christian. Others may decide that Christian commitment is not for them. The youth minister needs to recognize the fact that some young people will not take up the Christian aspect of this work. It is fundamental to Christian relational care that the youth minister will continue to be in relationship with a young person whether or not they decide to accept the Christian faith. In this way relational care becomes a sign of 'grace', that is the free gift of God's love in Christ. As such it is offered regardless of response.

MUTUALITY OF RELATIONSHIP

Relationships between the youth minister and young people have a balance and a mutuality to them. This is best seen in the way that youth ministers learn and grow by being in touch with young people. It is not the case that the adult youth minister is the 'provider' and that the young people are the receivers. Learning happens both ways.

This mutuality also affects the way that young people take up the Christian faith. The youth minister recognizes that young people need to work out what it is to be Christian in their own cultural and social settings. To follow Christ, therefore, is to be in relationship with God in a dynamic creative process. What Christian worship, morality and theology are is to be discovered as the young people read the Bible in the light of their context. This approach to Christian theology is called contextualization.[12]

RELATIONSHIP AND CHURCH

Young people who respond to the relationship offered by Christ will inevitably find support and encouragement from others who have followed a similar path. Groups of young people who share fellowship and worship with each other emerge wherever youth ministers offer relational care. These groups should be seen as embryonic church congregations which seek to express the faith within the particular context from which they have grown. In most cases, these groups should seek to grow into association with existing churches and denominations if they are to have an ongoing life. The network of friendships and contacts with young adults within the church, which often surrounds the work of the youth minister, can provide a supportive structure for this growing congregation. In many cases, the young adults involved see their own spirituality and church lives beginning to take on new allegiances and patterns of worship. In short, the young people and the young adults from the church start to develop a shared contextualized spirituality, and a church life together rooted in popular culture. Such a group has emerged in Oxford linked to St Clements Anglican Church; it is called JOY.[13]

Christian relational care: care

The youth minister is not primarily a counsellor, a sports coach, a musical director, a crisis manager, a careers advisor, an evangelist, or any other role we may care to think of. The youth minister is someone who is called to be in a caring relationship with young people. I am aware that in using the word 'care' I might just as easily substitute the biblical idea of Christian love or 'agape' (1 Corinthians 13:1–13). In my thinking these two terms are synonymous; however, for regular use in the context of youth ministry, the term 'care' is less open to misunderstanding.

THE LOVE OF GOD

An incarnational understanding of youth ministry finds its origins in the love or care that God has for his creation: 'For God loves the world so much that he sent his only Son' (John 3:16). God demonstrates in a concrete way his care for humanity by becoming human. It is this love of God which has taken hold of the youth minister and inspires him or her, in turn, to 'care' for young people.

The love of God is essentially relational. To be loved is to 'be known' intimately by someone. Being known is a trinitarian theme which has run throughout our work with young people.

⊙ **Being known by the Father.** When a group of young people got together to form a youth congregation in

Witney, they called themselves 'Root 139' because they were so inspired by the Psalm of the same number. These young people were deeply affected by the realization that God knew them intimately. This knowledge had a transforming effect on their lives. In this sense, it was powerful to be able to say with the psalmist, 'Lord you have examined me and you know me. You know everything I do' (Psalm 139:1).

⊙ **Being known by the Son.** A song written by a young person connected with Oxford Youthworks has worked its way deep into the spiritual lives of young people and adults alike.

> *You died on a wooden cross.*
> *With thorns on your head.*
> *Nails through your hands and feet.*
> *And a sword in your side.*
> *You tell me you understand.*
> *The thorns in my words.*
> *The nails that still pierce my heart*
> *And the sword through my soul.*[14]

The picture of a suffering Christ who identifies and understands the problems that we each face has consistently moved and renewed young people and youth ministers together as we worship.

⊙ **Being known by the Spirit.** One young person recently described her experience of God as a kind of 'rush' or a 'buzz'. These words, common in the drug scene, are used of an experience of God's Spirit. To be known by the Spirit physically in this way is exhilarating and energizing. One young person, who went through a similar experience, said to me, 'I don't believe in God, but something happened today which I can't explain.'

When the youth minister is in relationship with a young person offering care, he or she is an image or mirror of the trinitarian God. For the young person, the experience of care is a foretaste of being known by God who is Father, Son and Holy Spirit. The care offered by the youth minister finds its inspiration and point of reference from this basic Christian understanding of care.

RELATIONAL CARE

Just as God's care is made concrete through the willingness of Jesus to be in relationship with people, the youth minister also has to demonstrate care. Care is transmitted through the dynamic of relationships. In the first instance, the willingness on the part of the youth minister to be with young people on a consistent basis over a period of time, in and of itself is an expression of 'care'. Relationships, however, are also the forum within which the youth minister can exercise care by working with young people on issues, projects, joys, problems and opportunities as they arise. In this way, relationship mediates care. Care in this sense is extremely ordinary and everyday.

Care is also fundamentally related to the trust and respect that the youth minister offers to young people. In many cases this trust may be rejected or abused; however, the care offered by the youthworker needs to be forgiving and undaunted by the many set-backs and problems which arise. In this sense the respect and trust offered in friendship by the youth minister is a mirror of the way that God sees young people. It is, therefore, a sign of grace.

It is through 'grace' that each of us is enabled to bring about change in our lives. The youth minister who offers care does not act uncritically or without a concern to challenge young people to change their lifestyles or patterns of behaviour. Such change, however, grows out of a context of respect, understanding and trust. As young people seek to build mature and confident lives for themselves, the youth minister supports this process through care which does not shrink from challenging young people.[15]

Essential to challenging care is the integrity of the youthworkers themselves. Christian youthworkers should be clear about their own personal values and attitudes; and be willing to offer these in a sensitive and responsible way in conversations where young people seek advice or wish to know where we stand.

CARE AS SUPPORT

Young people are in transition from childhood to adulthood. This period of transition is one in which they are in need of friends to help them adjust to changes in sexuality, role, responsibility, and so on. Change and growth, at whatever period of life, involve uncertainty and risk. The primary responsibility of the youth minister is to be in relationship with young people as they undertake these changes. Care in the first place means that we are there as a supportive friend when they need one.

The youth minister, however, will also be there to work with young people when they are in crisis. Crisis can mean many different things to different young people. Crisis could include any one, or combination of, the following: homelessness, crime, bullying, family breakup, unplanned pregnancy, problems at school. Relational care is not a technique or method for dealing with such crises. Relational care means that the youth minister will be there in relationship with young people when they begin to experience problems of this sort. The youth minister then becomes a friend to whom they naturally turn when a crisis looms. Young people in crisis will also need particular kinds of support. Relational care ensures that the youth minister is on hand in the first instance to be the primary care worker in contact with the young person, but the youth minister will also be well-connected with other agencies, both Christian and statutory, in order that 'professional' help can be accessed by the young person with the minimum of problems. It is essential for the youth minister to be clear about the limitations of his or her role. The youth minister in situations of crisis will also be an adult friend who can support a young person as they come into contact with professional agencies.

RELATIONAL CARE CHANGES YOUNG PEOPLE

The youth minister is not primarily a problem solver, although in the course of caring he or she may help young people deal with particular problems. Similarly, the youth minister is not primarily an evangelist, although as a result of his or her care young people may very well start to respond to the love of Christ. The youth minister, in the first instance, is called to give him or herself in relationship to young people. This self-giving is itself the primary means by which young people are enabled to grow and develop. Relational care recognizes that young people are searching for a sense of self-worth and identity. The youth minister's main function in building relationships with young people is the recognition of the worth that is inherently there in each young person. At root, this worth comes from the youth minister's belief that this is the way that the young person is regarded by God. God loves every young person profoundly and passionately, and values them highly. In Christian theology, the value of each individual young person is expressed most profoundly in the death of Christ on the cross. Paul says, 'God has shown us how much he loves us— it was while we were sinners that Christ died for us!' (Romans 5:8). The paradox of the Christian faith is that God loves us and indeed is willing to demonstrate this love by his own self-sacrifice, even though we are not necessarily moral or religious people.

The task of the youth minister, who is in relationship with the young person, is to be a tangible demonstration of this divine care on a daily basis. It is our experience that such relationships have a powerful influence on young people's lives whether or not they decide to return God's love for them by becoming Christians. It is important to note that the youth minister does not bring self-worth to the young person, the youth minister simply recognizes the spiritual reality that God sees the young person as being of infinite worth. It is in relationship, therefore, that this self-worth is realized. A further consequence of this thinking is to challenge the view that the young person is of worth apart from a theological understanding of humanity. Christian relational care has as its basic premise the belief that care starts with the value that God places on people, rather than on a sense of human worth being a right of every human being.

CARING ENGENDERS COURAGE AND COURAGE LEADS TO FAITH

The relationship characterized by caring offered by the youth minister becomes a source of self-confidence for the young person. In relation to innumerable situations the youth minister, by his or her offer of support and encouragement, is able to work with young people to help them to achieve the things they want to achieve. This may be in sport, in relationships, with their family, with their friends, in their academic life, in connection with an addiction, in relation to criminal behaviour, in response to tragedy—the list is endless. Relationship, therefore, becomes the means by which young people are enabled to discover in themselves a courage to bring about change in their lives. Such change has within it the theological framework of repentance and faith.

In the first place, the young person may not recognize the 'spiritual' nature of the changes which they are engaged in bringing about in their own lives. The youth minister, however, will see that in many different ways, as the young person reaches towards growth and maturity, they are moving towards 'the good'. This movement towards 'the good' will be recognized by the youth minister as an echo of the kingdom of God. This does not mean that the young person is 'saved', or embraces Christ, or that they are ever going to be a part of the church. From the first the youth minister asks, 'What is it that God wills in the life of this particular young person at this moment in time?' Specific answers will differ but in general God wishes every young person to move towards 'the good', that is things that help the young person to develop into a mature and responsible adult, rather than 'the bad', that is things that prevent growth to maturity. To move towards 'the good' will also involve developing an attitude of respect for the good of others. To move towards 'the good' will involve an appreciation of corporate, community-based issues and a desire for justice.[16]

It is fundamental to Christian relational care that the youth minister recognizes that he or she does not have sole determination of what 'the good' might be. The youth minister, in truth, is also being challenged by God to embrace gospel values and concerns in his or her own life. Relational care, therefore, is characterized by a seeking together after God's will through prayer, worship and Bible study. It is important to recognize that to act as God wills in each specific cultural and social context will need to be worked out on a very practical and day-to-day basis. To care, therefore, will demand of the youthworker a particular sensitivity and willingness to learn and to grow with young people as they reveal their own cultural worlds. In the last instance, what is 'the good' in each circumstance will be defined by reference to Jesus, in the biblical record, and through a personal encounter in regular prayer, worship and action. It should be the goal of youth ministry that young people develop the ability to reach out in this way for 'the good' themselves. To be mature is to be able to define our own morality and responsibilities in the sight of God.[17]

This perspective does not deny the desire on the part of God to see young people eventually in relationship with him, and expressing this in service and worship. It simply is a recognition that God's concerns embrace the whole of a young person's life. God wishes to see young people grow as whole and healthy as they can possibly be. Ultimately, wholeness needs to involve some spiritual response to God in prayer and worship; however, at that time, the young person's concerns are echoed by God's care for the young person. The youth minister, in relationship with the young person, will be making this concern, or care, concrete to the young person by offering a relationship which supports him or her through change.

CARE MULTIPLIES

Youth ministers, in offering relational care, are following the prior care of God experienced in their own lives. As young people begin to grow in a caring environment, offered by the youth minister and their own friendship groups and family, they will begin to work on their own ability to care for others. The youth minister in this becomes a model, a guide and confidant to the young person. In this context, youth ministers will naturally be reflecting their own experience as Christians of the love of God in their own lives. The result of this sharing often means that young people begin to recognize that 'God is Love and whoever lives in love lives in union with God and God lives in union with him' (1 John 4:16). The experience of care and of giving care is profoundly spiritual. Indeed, in entering into caring relationships, the young person is meeting with the divine in the human.

Christian relational care will find ways to explore the relationship between the Christian message about Christ and the experience of care that the young people have come to. Some young people will respond to a God who cares for them and inspires them to care for other people. It is when this happens that the Christian community begins to emerge amongst them. Such a community will not be a 'buying' into already established Christian groups, although it may be a part of a church denomination, it will be a transformation of friendship networks that already exist between the young people involved. Such communities may well have links with a recognized 'church'; however, they will be characterized by organically evolving networks of relationship.[18]

CARE FOR GOD

Christian relational care will see as one of its goals young people readily responding to the care which God offers them. Care for God, or worship, involves the transformation of young people's social lives, future plans and cultural world. This transformation is distinct from traditional patterns of church life because it should avoid the imposition of middle-class cultural values, ways of relating and theological concerns. As such it is to be seen as truly indigenous, that is arising from the cultural frameworks of the young people themselves. Care for God in this sense will emerge as the young people themselves freely respond to the care that God has already made known in their own lives. It is in this context that we need to work towards alternative patterns of worship and liturgy that young people themselves develop.[19] These patterns of worship should not simply serve the church's need to have young people attending its buildings or becoming members of its denominations. Worship is the care that young people feel that they must offer to God because God first cared for them. In a similar way, care offered to God will also be expressed by young people as they give their lives in service. Such service is the worship every Christian offers to God.

For the youth minister, this care has been expressed in a calling to serve young people. The result of this care has been the establishment of groups of young people who, in their turn, will be listening to their own call to serve God in their community.

NOTES

1. This chapter is the second of three designed to explain the theory behind Oxford Youthworks. The other two papers are: 'The Case for a Contextualised Theology of Youth Sub-cultures' to be published in Ward and Lim *Adolescence, Youth Ministry and World Mission*, Paternoster and 'Distance and Closeness' published in *The Church and Youth Ministry*, edited by Pete Ward, Lynx, 1995b.

2. David Bosch, *Transforming Mission*, Orbis, 1992, p. 10.

3. John Stott, 'Imitating the incarnation', p. 57, from Comee and Guder *Readings in Incarnational Evangelism*, Young Life, 1985.

4. J. P. Leighton, *The Principles and Practice of Youth and Community Work*, 1972, p. 73.

5. Mark Smith, *Developing Youthwork*, 1988, pp. 1–9.

6. See Leonardo Boff, *Ecclesio-genesis*, Collins, 1986; Sione 'Amanaki Havea, *South Pacific Theology*, Regnum, 1987; Rosemary Radford Ruether, *Women Church*, Harper and Row, 1985; see also Pete Ward, *Youth Culture and the Gospel*, Harper Collins, 1992, pp. 22–45.

7. *The Alternative Service Book*, Oxford, 1980, p. 173.

8. See 'The Case for a Contextualised Theology of Youth Sub-Cultures' in Ward and Lim, 1995.

9. See Sam Adams 'Growing Up: The Inside World' in Ward, Adams and Levermore, *Youthwork and How to Do It*, Lynx, 1994, pp. 44ff.

10. Based on comments made by young people to Darren James.

11. These ideas suggested by Jude Levermore.

12. See Robert J. Schreiter, *Constructing Local Theologies*, SCM, 1985.

13. See Pete Ward, *Worship and Youth Culture*, Harper Collins, 1993.

14. Song lyrics, Copyright 1989, Ross MacDonald.

15. This point suggested by Sam Adams.

16. This point suggested by Sam Adams.

17. This point suggested by Sam Adams.

18. This point suggested by Hannah Barnes and Anna Chakka George.

19. See Ward, 1993.

2

The process of change through relationships between adults and young people

SAM ADAMS

Prepare the way for the Lord,
make straight paths for him.
Every valley shall be filled in, every mountain
shall be made low.
The crooked roads shall become straight,
the rough ways smooth.
And all mankind will see God's salvation.
LUKE 3:4, NIV

Adolescence is a period of change, of transition from childhood to adulthood. I wish to offer a framework for understanding the way in which positive relationships between Christian adults and young people can facilitate this change, create a climate within which this change can be healing and life-giving, and open a way for direct relationship with God.

This chapter, as you will discover, is a blend of theological reflection and psychology theory about adolescence, as viewed through the eyes of a practitioner. For the past few years I have been part of the Oxford Youthworks team, and this chapter reflects our shared doctrine, or framework, of Christian relational care as a basis for youth ministry. I recognize and value other frameworks, but choose to work and write within this one.

Human growth and development

Adolescence is a phase of life, part of a sequence of stages [1] through which we all negotiate a route on our personal journey between being knit together in the womb and the end of our earthly life. There is a developmental pattern which both defines our shared humanity (into which Christ entered when he was born as a baby) and which celebrates our uniqueness.

Just as snowflakes, although all formed in the same way and acted upon by the same general forces during their path to the earth, each have a beauty and design all their own, so it is with people. The unique moment of our creation, and the particular physical, emotional and spiritual experiences as we grow up and mature, form our individual expression of humanity. Here we see in action God's continued, detailed involvement in the life of his creation, hand in hand with the working out of the ground plan of that creation. Yet it is the commonality of experience, the general challenges of growing up and maturing, that enable us both to value this uniqueness and to identify with one another. Without these two key human abilities, the incarnation itself would be robbed of power. We would not be able to acknowledge the unique character of Christ, or make connections between his life and our own.

Adolescence

When I was a child, I talked like a child, I thought like a child, I reasoned like a child. When I became a man I put childish ways behind me.
1 CORINTHIANS 13:11, NIV

Adolescence is a particular phase in this process, characterized by some key issues associated with the transition from childhood to adulthood. The worlds of childhood, adolescence and adulthood are defined to some extent by external cultural, economic and political factors. In this discussion I will focus on the internal and interpersonal factors, assuming a 'Western' life experience, and leave for others the work of broadening the application of this framework to other cultures and taking into account such external factors as, for example, the experience of growing up in a war-zone.

Adolescence builds on the foundations of earlier life stages, it never happens in a void. The particular tasks of this stage are connected to preparation for adulthood: responding to the physical and emotional challenges of puberty, achieving a firm yet flexible enough identity on which to build adult life and psychologically separating from the family as the predominant source of care and support. At the same time, if this phase goes well enough, there is the opportunity for the first time in life to go back over old ground, to reshape and redefine old experiences before launching into the new world of adulthood. These four tasks (puberty, identity, separation and recapitulation) will be discussed in turn later, looking at the positive role an adult Christian friend can offer.

Being-in-relatedness

I have come in order that you might have life—life in all its fulness.
JOHN 10:10, GNB

Life is a gift born out of relationship. The poverty or richness of our lives is a reflection of the quality of the relationships in our lives; relationships with present and absent others, relationships with the persons of the trinity. Behind the ground plan of growth, in stages as life progresses, lies a God-given dynamic of relationship, of one coming to another in order that they might have life in its fulness.

Frank Lake developed a model in the late 1950s of personal and spiritual health and wholeness, describing the dynamics of relationship which form and maintain this.[2] This model takes as its definition of normal humanity neither the average of human experience nor a theoretical norm, but the life of Christ.[3] Thus normal humanity becomes what God intended, that which existed prior to the fall, and which is available again now through the redemptive work of Christ.

Frank Lake applied the model of 'the dynamic cycle of being' to the clinical and research findings concerning the first year of life in particular. I wish to use his model to describe the interpersonal dynamic of incarnational youth ministry. At Oxford Youthworks, we have long acted upon a collective assumption that care engenders courage, and courage enables young people to change and move towards 'the good'.[4] This model helps to provide a theoretical framework to describe and examine our experience.

The dynamic cycle of being

The normal (that is, ideal) pattern of interpersonal relationships can be described as consisting of four factors, in dynamic relationship to one another and in sequence—as shown by the four sides of a quadrilateral. The width of the passage indicates the increase and diminishment of the 'powers of being'.

THE DYNAMIC INPUT PHASE

⊙ Acceptance by a significant other or others is the way in. This access to human relationships ensures, on the personal level, one's very 'being'. Without this, one 'dies' as a person or as a member of society. Personal life is possible only when the seeking 'I' finds a 'Thou'.[5] This alone makes possible the emergence of selfhood, of a steadily functioning identity.[6]

Lord, you have searched me and you know me.
PSALM 139:1, NIV

The personal source comes down to the person waiting in need.

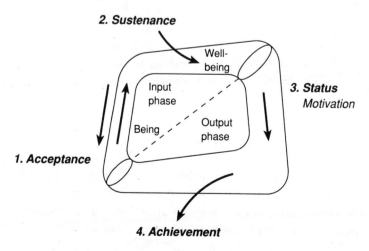

2. **Sustenance**

Well-being

Input phase

3. **Status**
Motivation

Being

Output phase

1. **Acceptance**

4. **Achievement**

This is my own dear son, whom I love; with him I am well pleased.
MATTHEW 3:17, NIV

Father, I thank you that you have heard me, I know that you always hear me.
JOHN 11:41, NIV

⊙ Sustenance of personality. Whoever enjoys relationships of a generous and gracious kind is enhanced by them in their power of 'being'. The quality of 'well-being', good spirits, courage and personal vitality, is a reflection of what has been communicated from self-giving others in this phase. 'Well-being' is achieved by responding to all the good things on offer in the relationship.

God gives the Spirit without limit.
JOHN 3:34, NIV

Just as the living Father sent me and I live because of the Father, so the one who feeds on me will live because of me.
JOHN 6:57, NIV

Now to him who is able to do immeasurably more than all we ask or imagine, according to his power that is at work within us.
EPHESIANS 3:20, NIV

THE DYNAMIC OUTPUT PHASE

⊙ Status as a loved and satisfied person. The two ingoing dependency phases are followed by an outgoing movement, back to involvement in self-giving relationships in the place where tasks are taken up. This is the way out to freedom from dependency and to selfhood. The natural desire is to care for others as they have been cared for, to love as they have been loved. The quality of spirit that has been induced by the experiences of the first two phases is passed on to others. The person is in good heart, and is able to enjoy, as a gift which has not been earned, the status of a courageous person. Courageous ethical motivation is felt here.

As the Father has loved me, so have I loved you.
JOHN 15:9, NIV

When the Holy Spirit comes upon you, you will be filled with power, and you will be witnesses for me.
ACTS 1:8, GNB

⊙ Achievement of tasks appropriate to the person. Purposeful activity is required of every human being in society, whether it be the acquisition of skills in childhood or the performance of work and service in adult life. This involves the expenditure of the income from earlier phases of the dynamic cycle. Work is done with sustained application and concentration, with fair tolerance of frustration, with realistic adjustment to difficulties, but with steady persistence of aim. Personal relationships with others are characterized by outgoingness, openness, generosity, kindness, tact, warmth and reliability of commitment, peacefulness, hopefulness and patience.

My food is to obey the will of the one who sent me and to finish the work he gave me to do.
JOHN 4:34, GNB

Therefore, since we are surrounded by such a great cloud of witnesses, let us throw off everything that

*hinders and the sin that so easily entangles, and let us
run with perseverance the race marked out for us.*
HEBREWS 12:1, NIV

*The fruit of the Spirit is love, joy, peace, patience,
kindness, goodness, faithfulness, gentleness and self-
control.*
GALATIANS 6:22, NIV

The youth minister as source person

The source person within the dynamic cycle is the one who
comes to give acceptance and sustenance. As youth ministers
we seek to build real, life-enhancing relationships of depth
and length with young people. When we enter the worlds of
young people, we need to do so as good source people, able
to offer what is needed for being and well-being, and willing
to deal with the response of those to whom we offer this.

In view of the needs of adolescents, the tasks of their life
stage, it is very important that we are in fact adults, and not
adolescents in disguise. We need to have already charted
this territory for ourselves, to have satisfactorily resolved
the issues of puberty, identity, separation and recapitulation.
If not, we are in danger of being blind leaders and, as Jesus
said, 'When one blind man leads another, both fall into a
ditch' (Matthew 15:14, GNB).

As would-be helpers, we need to be committed to our own
personal and spiritual health, maintained through our own
positive, dynamic relationships with our fellows and God. We
also need to keep a healthy contact with our own humanly
inescapable feelings of guilt, weakness, longing, anger,
anxiety, despair and the like, as well as joy, tenderness,
reconciliation and peace, if we are to be able to accept and
stay with whatever may emerge from the young person.

The treasure we carry and offer to the young people to
whom we minister is the Good News of right-relationships

through Christ. 'Yet we who have this spiritual treasure are like common clay pots, in order to show that the supreme power belongs to God, not to us' (2 Corinthians 4:7). It is our very flawed humanity that points to the divine and infinite resource on which we depend.

In our engagement in the lives of young people, we need to be committed to their growth towards holistic maturity: adult life in its fulness. This must include an inner ability to accept and sustain oneself (although we never become entirely self-dependent), so as to make positive sense of Christ's command to 'love our neighbours as ourselves'. This intention is vital if we are to avoid making young people dependent upon us, to avoid youth ministry becoming a permanent substitute for the family as a hiding place from adult life. Our long-term desire should be to see them no longer need us, indeed for it to be perhaps 'better for them if we go', so that they can engage fully in adult life as our equals, choosing to give and receive in many dynamic relationships.

Our motivation and model for engaging in relationship with young people is Christ, and this is ultimately a model of self-sacrifice. Christian ministry costs its ministers, yet the rewards are incomparable.

> *Blessed are those who hunger and thirst for right-relationships, for they will be filled...*
>
> *Blessed are those who are persecuted for the sake of right-relationships, for theirs is the kingdom of heaven.*
> MATTHEW 5:6, 10[7]

The process of change through relationships

Within the dynamic cycle, much of the impetus for movement and change lies with the source person; the young person can hardly respond to what is not present. The challenge of youth ministry is to take the task of building relationships with young people in this dynamic way out of the church and into the life of the community.

ACCEPTANCE

The youth minister sets out to find young people, to go to them, to their home turf, thereby showing acceptance through a willingness to come near. To seek to know and be known. Unconditional love is mediated by spending time, giving attention. The skills of active listening and empathy are needed here. There are clear correlations here with the core conditions necessary for effective counselling and other professional helping relationships.[8]

SUSTENANCE

This phase is about recognizing and responding appropriately to need. This may be practical and even mundane, but it is a moving on from acceptance to a deeper level of relating. The love offered, on the firm foundation of unconditional love, now incorporates a more conditional love: I love you more if you respond from 'the good' in you, if you do what pleases God.[9] Care may be a more useful word here than love. Care is not neutral: it wants the best for the cared-for-one, it mourns with, or rejoices with, the cared-for one. Sustenance must build up, be of the truth and, therefore, will offer critique and challenge to the receiver.

STATUS

Here the dynamic changes from input to output. The youth minister demonstrates his or her trust and belief in the young people by letting them risk and discover that they have the courage to do so. Young people often verbalize their status by naming the relationship in some way. At Oxford Youthworks we find young people, with no prompting from the Christian adults they know, begin to call themselves Christians, to name their status with God.

ACHIEVEMENT

Young people need opportunities to give, to contribute meaningfully to the life of their communities, to expend their selves in the service of others. Sometimes youth ministers need to act to help create a climate in which this is possible, and need also to be willing to receive from the young people with whom they are engaged in dynamic relationships.

A number of studies of secular helping professions have shown that what makes an effective helper is a consequence of the helper's belief system (rather than the model or method they employ), particularly their beliefs about empathy, self, what people are like and the helper's purposes.[10] This model of dynamic relationships starts with an explicitly Christ-centred belief system. As a source person, the youth minister offers to the young person his or her faith, self and love. Let us now look at the needs of young people specific to adolescence, and the role a relationship with a caring Christian adult can play.

Puberty

Adolescence is marked by the physical changes associated with puberty, and the onset of genital maturity. Interest in sexuality increases, along with anxieties about one's own normality and attractiveness. In this minefield of teenage hormones and emotions, a safe and trustworthy adult friend can help. A safe person on whom to test one's attractiveness (that is, flirt), a trustworthy confidant for one's anxieties, as well as a source of trustworthy information concerning taboo and superstition-riddled subjects.

Identity

It is in adolescence that we construct our basic framework of who we are,[11] from the raw materials available to us: our past, our culture and setting, and our present dynamic relationships. J. E. Marcia has proposed a useful model for defining identity status in adolescence.[12] In essence, this uses two criteria: has there been any serious consideration of alternatives or crisis? and has there been any commitment to identity? This gives four possible status positions.

By 'identity crisis' Marcia means some serious consideration of alternative possibilities, such as ideologies or life goals. This may or may not be a traumatic experience. By 'committed to identity' he means a relatively firm choice of a specific identity.

The four different statuses are defined by these two sets of criteria. Individuals in the Identity Achievement group have gone through a period of crisis and have developed relatively firm commitments. Individuals in the Moratorium group are currently in a state of crisis and are actively exploring and seeking to make identity-related choices.

Identity Status
(Marcia)

committed to identity

		YES	NO
identity crisis	**YES**	Identity Achievement	Moratorium
	NO	Foreclosure	Diffusion

Individuals in the Foreclosure group have never experienced a crisis, although they have committed themselves to particular goals and values which generally reflect the wishes of authority figures. Individuals in the Identity Diffusion group do not have firm commitments and are not actively exploring or trying to form any commitments; these adolescents or adults may or may not have been through a crisis period, but there has been no clear resolution of their identity or commitments.

Diffusion is most likely to occur as a result of inadequate dynamic relationships in earlier childhood, so we shall concentrate on foreclosure and moratorium as more 'normal' adolescent statuses, with identity achievement as the goal. Jesus tells a story of two suitably adolescent brothers (Luke 15:11–32). The younger enters moratorium, actively exploring new experiences and seeking to make identity-related choices, and returns on his way to identity achievement. The elder one demonstrates his foreclosure by his disapproval, revealing that his identity is committed to what he assumes are the wishes of the authority figures in his life. The key to this story is the role of the father or source person. With each of the brothers, he positively invites them up to the status of identity achievement. To the younger brother, he offers the status of son rather than servant, and celebrates his response to this. To the older brother, he offers a fuller understanding of his status as son, rather than the status he has assumed of glorified servant: 'You are always here with me, and everything I have is yours' (Luke 15:31, GNB).

Therefore, youth ministers can also extend invitations to the status of identity achievement to young people. As our ministry arises from our own being-in-relatedness with Christ, our understanding of identity achievement cannot be complete without discovering our identity in Christ, and here, too, we must be willing to extend the invitation.

As young people move towards identity achievement, we can act as a constant reference point for them to bang forcibly against, or to stand at a distance from, in order to gain their own bearings. Being in close relationship with young people as they pass through moratorium can provoke and challenge us. This may be a gift of pure gold that has passed through the refining fire of crisis, if we are willing to receive it. In this way, a young person in 'crisis' may push us in an area that we had previously 'foreclosed', opening up the opportunity for us to grow as well.

Erikson suggests that a vital by-product of the development of identity is the virtue of 'fidelity'—a new-found ability to be faithful to, or sustain commitment to, a person, idea, opinion or cause. Young people are looking for ideas, opinions, theories and people worth believing in, worth basing their very selves upon and being faithful to. As source people, youth ministers actively model fidelity to Christ.

Separation

Adolescents are involved in the psychological struggle of separating from their familiar source of care and support, the family, and venturing out into society as more independent individuals. For many, this is a see-saw of needing parental support, yet fearing that to take succour from that source might sap their ability to separate successfully. Here a youth minister can find a young person choosing to use them as a surrogate parent, a safe relationship within which to receive parental-type care, without the fear of being engulfed by it and trapped in the world of childhood dependency.

Recapitulation

Adolescence is the first opportunity (there may be others) not only to complete the tasks of this stage, but also to rework previous stages. This will only be possible if there are more than sufficient resources available during adolescence, that is if the young person is in positive dynamic relationships. This recapitulation of old themes is part of God's common grace, a source of healing available to believers and non-believers alike.

This may happen in a number of ways, for example by the young person consciously or unconsciously seeking out 'substitute experiences'[13] through current relationships. John Cleese talks of his lack of experience of firm discipline from his father, and his teenage decision to join the army. Sacrament is another key, the active remembering and reliving of events of significance to enable them to be incorporated into the present. Regression to earlier ways of reacting and behaving is a common outworking of this process, and youth ministers need to be able to recognize and value this.

P. Blos suggests that even those exposed to the kindliest of childhood fates have innumerable opportunities for emotional injury. Reworking and mastering this 'trauma' is a life-long task; resolution is not removing the trauma, but rather finding satisfying ways to cope with what was originally an unmanageable childhood ordeal. Adolescence, because of its role in the consolidation of character, is a time when 'a considerable portion of this task is being accomplished'.[14] It is recapitulation that enables us as adults to have access to the child within, without which we cannot gain entry to paradise:

I tell you the truth, unless you change and become like little children, you will never enter the kingdom of heaven.
MATTHEW 18:3, NIV

Dynamic relationships as mission

The purpose of dynamic relationships is to participate in God's mission to his creation. These dynamic relationships are modelled on, and point to, the dynamic relationship God the Father, through Christ, desires to have with each of his created beings.

I tell you the truth, whoever accepts anyone I send accepts me; and whoever accepts me accepts the one who sent me.

JOHN 13:20, NIV

This is the Good News. Living in right and positive dynamic relationships with God and his people is justification by faith through grace. Dynamic relationships make a seamless robe of evangelism and pastoral care. Indeed, the dynamic relationships of Christ's human ministers are the response to being in such relationship with Christ, the output and overflow of received acceptance and sustenance. We are called to be source persons:

Let me tell you why you are here. You're here to be salt-seasoning that brings out the God-flavours of this earth. If you lose your saltiness, how will people taste godliness?... You're here to be light, bringing out the God-colours in the world. God is not a secret to be kept... Be generous with your lives. By opening up to others you'll prompt people to open up with God, this generous Father in heaven.

MATTHEW 5:13–16[15]

This calling is a challenge to the whole body of the church, not the preserve of a few 'specialists'. The church should be looking to encourage all Christian adults to be youth ministers. A theology of adulthood and identity achievement in Christ is needed. At a more grass roots level, Christian adults need to know that they have something invaluable to offer young people. All should be empowered to offer dynamic relationships to the young people that they know.

Adolescence is a crucial time when such relationships are much needed. It is also, for many young people, the first time in their lives when they are in a position to have some choice about who they relate to.

This leaves the question of the many young people who are not known by Christian adults, whose lives do not naturally bring them into contact with them. For Christian adults to offer acceptance and sustenance to these young people, who are so very different from themselves, there needs to be training and resources which recognize both the challenges of the context (culture, and so on) and the challenges of building dynamic relationships across the generations.

As youth ministers, let us take our mandate from John the Baptist. Our task is to prepare the way for the Lord. We are to do this through dynamic relationships with young people which fill in valleys of need; make low shrines to falseness in high places; straighten crooked concepts of justice and right-relationships; and smooth rough scars, responses and reactions to old unrighteousness. If we, with the grace of God, are able to do this within and outside the church, all mankind will truly see God's salvation.

As the Father sent me, so I send you.
JOHN 20:21, GNB

NOTES

1. See E. H. Erikson, *Childhood and Society*, W. W. Norton and Co. Inc., 1963; *Identity, Youth and Crisis*, 1968; J. C. Coleman and L. Hendry, *The Nature of Adolescence*, Routledge, 1990.

2. Frank Lake, *Clinical Theology*, abridged, Yeomans, Darton, Longman and Todd, 1986.

3. See Barth for discussion of Christ as ideal.

4. Pete Ward, 'Christian relational care', above.

5. Martin Buber, *I and Thou*.

6. Modern philosophy argues that all thought is framed in language, which assumes communication and relationship.

7. I am highlighting one aspect of Matthew's use of the term 'righteousness'—this incorporates right-relations, right attitudes and a setting of things to right.

8. See, for example, R. R. Carkhuff, *Helping and Human Relations* (volume 2), Holt Rinehart and Winston, 1969; and D. Mearns and B. Thorne, *Person-Centred Counselling in Action*.

9. See Eric Fromm's description of mother love and father love in *The Art of Loving*.

10. See the summary of findings in Arthur W. Combs, 'What Makes a Good Helper?', *Person-Centred Review*, Sage, February 1986.

11. See Sam Adams, 'Growing Up: The Inside World' in Ward, Adams and Levermore, *Youthwork and How to Do It*, Lynx Communications, 1994.

12. J. E. Marcia, for example 'Identity in Adolescence' in J. Adelson (ed.) *Handbook of Adolescent Psychology*, Wiley, 1980.

13. John Cleese and Robin Skynner, *Families and How to Survive Them*.

14. P. Blos, *On Adolescence: A Psychoanalytic Interpretation*, Free Press, 1962.

15. Eugene H. Peterson, *The Message*, Navpress, 1993.

3

Change through peer relationships

STEVE TILLEY

Adolescence is a minefield of change. Those who stomp around in minefields are likely to end up maimed. The safe route through a minefield is slow, laborious and analytical. In this chapter I am going to walk optimistically though the middle of the minefield. I think I know a route through. It may not be the only route but, let's face it, if you know a safe way through a minefield it is sensible to use it rather than investigate alternatives.

In his book *Understanding Adolescence,*[1] Dr Roger Hurding identifies eleven areas of change that a young teenager must expect to face: change in body, identity, image, lifestyle, relationship with parents, relationship with peers, morals, emotions, behaviour, situations and loyalties. Those of us who have a heart for teenage evangelism desperately want to avoid manipulating young people at a time when these changes render them very susceptible to outside influences, but we do want to give them an opportunity to hear, and respond to, the gospel.

So what sort of change are we talking about in this chapter? I will eventually interpret it quite narrowly as, 'Growing in Christian maturity', but to begin with I want to talk about change more generally.

How does change take place through peer relationships? I will try and answer both experientially and technically.

I can remember my own teenage years quite vividly. Talking to friends and colleagues I have discovered that my own experience of being a teenager was a fairly common one. Although quite capable of being open and intimate within individual relationships, time spent in larger groups, like classes at school, was about survival. Survival meant not being the one who was put down, the subject of jokes, bullying and abuse. To stay in with the in-crowd you had to be quick-witted and able to contribute. The aim was not to be the loudest or the quietest, nor the most badly behaved or the saint, but to strive for acceptable anonymity.

During this time there were a number of key people who influenced me. If there was someone I respected I would try to be like them. More to the point I would try to get them to like me. I still recoil from the rather complicated lie I told a friend to convince him that I had been at a particular midweek football match which my Mum and Dad had barred me from attending. I couldn't bring myself to admit that I hadn't been there. The shame would have been too great.

I believe that change through peer relationships happens because we all go through life copying those pieces of social behaviour that impress us and rejecting those that don't.

Well the cocaine club says welcome
You're in college now not school...
But I don't want to be like that
No I don't want to be like that.

JOE JACKSON[2]

The task of the church-based youth leader is to help the young people in the group to live lives that are worth copying. We must '... be prepared to give an answer to everyone who asks you to give the reason for the hope that you have'(1 Peter 3:15). The only reason people will ask us to do this is if they see something in our behaviour that impresses them.

Today, nearly a quarter of a century on from my mid-teens, I still observe young people striving for acceptable anonymity. There have always been those who want to be outrageous; to stand out in a crowd. They are the tribal leaders. Others just want to belong. My own twelve-year-old son attends a school which has no uniform. He spends a great deal of time making sure he looks just right before he leaves home in the morning. 'Just right' means, as far as I can see, looking exactly the same as the others in his year. They have a uniform of their own creation. My older son goes to a different school. It has a uniform. He has perfected the art of minimizing the gap between leaving his bed and leaving the house. The uniform is thrown on. He doesn't worry about it. I am not making a school uniform point here. I am ambivalent on the subject. I am making the point that young people strive to belong and this is typified by the way they dress. My personal search for a red, skinny-fit, Brutus round-collared shirt in 1969 is matched by my son's search for an extra-large black, Pearl Jam T-shirt in 1994. Funnily enough we both wanted black Doc Martens, so at least one firm has got the teenage footwear market sorted.

Experience tells me that young people want to conform to each other in order either to rebel against their parents' generation, or simply to assert their own independence. Change takes place as those who market products associated with fashion, music and leisure try to manipulate their product into first place in teen popularity. As soon as a new product hits the streets, and two or three people are doing it, wearing it or listening to it, the manufacturers can prepare for a few months of excellent sales. If this were not true there would be no advertising. Change is rapid and often short-lived. A generation in youthwork is often as short as six months. As someone said, 'the only thing that is true is that if it is "in", it is on the way out.'

Teenagers will latch onto good models as well as bad. Today there are many teenagers anxious to save the planet, feed the starving and see animals treated humanely, to name but three topical issues. Much of the interest in these issues has been generated by peer relationships. That is the experiential answer. What of the technical?

There have been many studies by behavioural scientists into patterns of conformity. The pioneering work by such as Solomon Asch[3] established that even on a simple test, where a normal respondent would regularly score 99 per cent, as few as three or four people primed to give an incorrect response could persuade the subject to change their mind and answer incorrectly. The television personality James Burke repeated this experiment during the course of a scientific series on BBC in the 1970s. The results were more pronounced. People are frightened of non-conformity and the idea of being the odd person out, especially on television, frightened subjects into conformity.

Why should this be? There are three possible reasons why we like to conform. The first is that of compliance. We accept influence from another person because we either seek rewards or aim to avoid punishment. This goes some way towards explaining my behaviour at school. I saw the reaction to our social outcasts. I didn't want to be treated like that so I tried to conform to avoid the punishment.

The second reason is classification. This describes an individual's willingness to associate themselves with another person or group because that relationship gives them self-definition. The relationship becomes part of the person's self-image. This might just be the reason why I am happy to be seen as a West Bromwich Albion fan, although others have suggested it must be because someone dropped me on my head when I was a kid.

The third reason is congeniality. The individual adopts the values of another either to solve a problem or to maximize their own values. This is the most selfish of motives for change. I am looking to do the best I can for myself. I see in somebody else some quality that will help me on the way and so I adopt it for as long as is necessary to achieve my aims. If necessary I adopt it permanently and live with the self-deception, thereby becoming a candidate for therapy in the future should relationships fall apart around me. Notice George Michael's apparently autobiographical lyrics from 'Freedom 90'.

I think there's something you should know
I think it's time I told you so
There's something deep inside of me
There's someone else I've got to be...[4]

The first part of my route through the minefield is to acknowledge that teenagers will be profoundly influenced by their peers. Asking a young person to be the only Christian in their class at school is asking a very difficult thing of them. But if there are two or three the task becomes much easier and the possibilities for evangelism greater. A wise youth leader once told me the secret of numerical growth in his group. 'Aim to have ten young people and more boys than girls,' he said, 'and the group will grow almost despite you.' I remembered this the first time I took on the leadership of a small group in a church. It encouraged me because the group I inherited had ten boys and two girls. By the time I handed it on to new leaders there were twenty-five regularly attending on a Sunday and they had demanded a midweek Bible study as well. Peer relationships are a powerful ally in the work of growing a youth group.

I now work as the Head of the Church Youth Fellowships' Association—known to many simply as CYFA. We don't claim to be the best Christian youthwork agency. We don't want to know if we are the biggest, because comparing numbers is inappropriate. All we can say is that we have grown in popularity. In 1983 we had contact with 711 groups. This figure passed 1,000 in 1989 and by 1994 we were trying to support 1,194 affiliated groups. I'm naturally suspicious of statistics, but I think it's true to say we've grown.

Mark Ashton was Head of CYFA from 1981–87. He identified five principles on which church-based youthwork ought to be grounded:

⊙ Belief in the power of prayer as the mainstay of youthwork.

⊙ Belief in the power of the Bible as the backbone of the teaching programme.

⊙ Belief in the power of the simple gospel as the central attraction of youthwork.

⊙ Belief in the importance of the individual as the practical guideline for the pastoring of the group.

⊙ Belief in the fellowship of the Body as the necessary context for growth for a young Christian.[5]

Our ultimate aim can be expressed as Paul put it in Colossians 1:28, '... so that we may present everyone perfect in Christ.' We want to present young people as perfect in Christ, or 'mature in Christ' as some versions of the Bible put it. Because we live in the expectation of Jesus' return, we don't know the day or the hour on which this presentation will take place and so there is urgency in our work.

Until the day of Christ's return how ought this maturity express itself? I believe we need to present young people as full adult members of the church when they reach the age at which society recognizes them as adults. In other words, we hope that at eighteen years old, a young adult will identify with the whole church, not just the group in which their faith has been nurtured. Furthermore, we hope that they will be able to contribute to society as a mature, Christian adult.

The CYFA staff try to encourage affiliated groups to work to these principles. We want youth leaders to stay alongside teenagers throughout all the tumultuous changes of adolescence. The result is a group of leaders who are content to work with small groups of young people. Whilst numerical growth is desirable it is not set up as a greater desire than personal, spiritual growth. Discipling a new Billy Graham might have greater consequences than converting 1,000 at a youth service. Mark Ashton identifies this as the method chosen by Jesus; '... there was a clear focus in Jesus' method. While he must have touched the lives of a great many people, he was content to make a significant impact on the lives of just a few.'[6] He also points to this being the pattern in the rest of the New Testament. 'Like Jesus, Paul travelled with a small band of companions with whom he shared his life. When he found himself separated from them, he suffered great distress (see 2 Timothy 4:9–22).'[7] Furthermore, he suggests that this is consistent with the Old Testament model of faith communication. 'Faith is to be communicated as a life-commitment by adults who act as models to the young.'[8]

This challenges us. If we are modelling the Christian life to young people then we ought to be modelling personal evangelism as something that we do with our friends. We ought to be involved in ongoing, long-term relationships with people who are not yet Christians. If the only people the youth pastor ever communicates the gospel to are young people, then those same young people will smell a rat when asked to be evangelists themselves. They will assume it is something that is done for them, not by them.

So, the second part of my route through the minefield is the reminder that if I haven't got any friends who are not Christians, I ought to stop what I am doing and go out and get some. Assuming I have done this, I can return to the world of young people.

What are young adolescents like? It is a brave author who attempts to tackle this question in half a paragraph. It has occupied the minds of the thesis-writing public for years.[9] It is certainly true that young people have the capacity for over-exuberance and great melancholy, dedicated confidentiality and petty jealousy, incisive wisdom and incredible stupidity; the frustration of youthwork is that these reactions can all come in the space of about twenty minutes. I enjoyed my friend's observation that a youthworker must be a person with an endless capacity for disappointment.

Many young people are certainly fearful, frustrated, fed up with listening and bottled up. I don't know if this is true of every adolescent. I am describing Elihu, Job's fourth comforter, the one who spoke last because he was the youngest (Job 32:6–22). It is certainly a danger in youthwork that if all the significant relationships are adult/young person then the young person will identify the youth leader as an authority figure only; either as a parent or as a teacher. One group of young people I heard about, asked to rewrite Psalm 23 in their own language, came up with, 'The Lord is my Probation Officer.' Strong peer relationships prevent young people from becoming fearful and bottled up. If the only relationship deemed to be of any importance is that between the youth leader and the young people, they are bound to feel frustrated.

In some churches the appointment of a full-time youth pastor is a sign not of interest in youthwork but of abdication of it. All the weight of congregational frustration with young people is dumped on one poor soul who is expected to lead, train, excite, enthuse and instruct the young people, and is also the focus of all conversations with them. Consequently all communication between older and younger people in the church happens through the youth minister. When I was a youth minister I refused point blank to take responsibility for such requests as, 'Would you ask the young people to stop blocking the doorway.' I would make people talk to the young people themselves, even if it was to complain. Thankfully it was a church where young people were taken seriously, for the most part, so there were fewer difficulties than I have experienced in some other places. But we must accept that young people like to be in groups of young people. It is great to encourage young and old to mix at church meetings. It will not be easy and it will not be natural for the young people. If it is forced upon them too regularly they may leave. It is far easier to leave a youth group you attend voluntarily than a family or a classroom. Far better to invest some time and training in good peer relationships so they can encourage, train and yes, even counsel, each other, than to be loaded down with the weight of being the only one who can take pastoral care of young people.[10]

If strong peer relationships are desirable, how can they be achieved? The beauty of this is that they don't have to be achieved. Young people will develop friendships. Indeed their behaviour will be almost tribal. As we have seen, a group of peers will have cultural distinctives to do with their taste in music, clothes and leisure, but school groupings break down a lot of these barriers. Schools are an important ally.

If a church-based group builds on the existing relationships between the members and their friends it will be a basis for evangelism. Of course, there will be times when it is appropriate to put on particular evangelistic events, but these will be occasional. The basic methodology of building evangelism into existing relationships is that friends are welcome to any group meeting and inviting them is encouraged. It doesn't make a dramatic difference to the programme. The core programme is still to introduce the group to biblical truth. I believe that if this is done in the presence of Christians it is discipleship, and if it is done in the presence of those who are not Christians it is evangelism. If both are present, then it is both. The line between evangelism and discipleship is not easy to draw, if indeed there is one.

Some churches use special interest groupings to begin the process of evangelism. This might be through a church football team, a drama group or an interest in a particular type of music.

Peer groups are places of trust, influence and pressure. A supportive peer group maximizes the first two and releases the third. The youth leader will be able to provide a discipline and a syllabus. Being a place of safety, the group will generate questions and be able to discuss important issues of the Christian life. A small age range of, say, fourteen to eighteen will enable older peers to model the Christian life to the younger members of the group. The younger ones will discover that it is possible to remain a Christian in the Sixth Form, at College, at work or on the dole. The older ones will begin to exercise leadership, perhaps in small group studies, in prayer times or in worship. They will be exposed to leadership in front of a supportive group. I thank CYFA/Pathfinder Ventures for the summer, Easter and New Year house parties at which I learned most of what was helpful for Christian ministry. A large part of the reason for their success was the presence of a narrow age range in front of which I felt comfortable doing leadership for the first time.

Older members are also able to demonstrate a certain stickability. Not everyone in the youth group is destined for leadership. It has been a criticism of some Christian youthwork in the past that young people are left with nothing to do but to try and lead the group. Those who cannot lead often demand a group for eighteen- to twenty-five-year-olds and everyone proceeds through their church life in generation groupings. But this is not a sign of Christian maturity. The mature Christian is comfortable in a multi-generational environment.

And that is the final part of the route through. It is simple to state and onerous to put into practice. It is not to decry other methods of youthwork. To stay with the metaphor I began with, there are other minefields. There will be young people who are outside the scope of the tribes to which all your church's young people belong. I don't believe that quite as many are out of reach as is sometimes suggested. I have heard it said that up to 85 per cent of this country's young people are beyond the reach of church-based youthwork. This is ridiculous. Just because they have not been reached does not make them out of reach. Last week a spoon fell down the back of my fridge. I know how to get it back but it requires a time commitment I cannot offer at present. I'll get it in the end. Reaching young people beyond the fringe of your present church youthwork may require the help of professionals and a time commitment which the volunteer youth leader can probably not give.

Nevertheless, I believe that young people themselves are the best evangelists for young people and if a church has only limited resources to put into youthwork these are well used in encouraging a small group to take the Bible seriously. A church that takes youthwork seriously will still be a church in ten years time. The Bible is God's unchanging word to a changing world. A church that takes the Bible seriously in its youthwork will have leaders in ten years time.

NOTES

1. Dr Roger Hurding, *Understanding Adolescence*, Hodder and Stoughton, 1989.

2. Joe Jackson, 'Don't Wanna Be Like That' from *I'm the Man*, A & M Records, 1979.

3. Solomon Asch, 'Opinions and Social Pressure: Papers in Socialization and Attitudes', *Scientific American*, 1974.

4. George Michael, 'Freedom 90' from *Listen Without Prejudice*, Epic Records, 1990.

5. Mark Ashton, 'Where Are We Going? (Thinking About Basics)', A resource paper from CYFA, 1983.

6. Mark Ashton, *Christian Youthwork*, Kingsway, 1986, p. 97.

7. Ashton, *Christian Youthwork*, p. 97.

8. Ashton, 'Where Are We Going?', p. 95.

9. Those wishing to read more on this subject might like to look at Pete Gilbert's *Understanding Teenagers*, Crossway, 1993 or Hurding's *Understanding Adolescence*.

10. A helpful guide to this is in *Peer Counselling in Youth Groups* by Joan Sturkie and Siang-Yang Tan, 1992 in Zondervan's Youth Specialties series.

4

Evangelism among pre-Christian young people

BOB MAYO

How can we be so wrong?

I have lost count of the amount of times I have been told about someone or other, who has lived in the inner city for twenty-five years and developed a superb culturally relevant church; or about someone, who has written a PhD on the subject of evangelism in East Clacton 1972–76 (for example); or someone else, who has written a book on the subject of gospel presentation to third-generation Afro-Caribbeans living in Peckham and aged between forty and sixty-five.

The assumption behind all of these types of conversations is that when we talk about 'Jesus' people will understand what we are talking about, even if they don't agree; if Christianity is presented well enough—in a culturally relevant or accessible manner—then people might not agree, but they will at least understand what it is that they are hearing. This assumption is wrong.

However, this assumption is still held in most books on evangelism. The reality is that 47 per cent of people in the country have not heard the basic Christian story. Of the remaining 53 per cent, who have heard something of the Christian message, many have formed negative impressions and wrong conclusions about the Christian faith.

The use of any language takes for granted the idea that people know what the word being used means—a vicar is visiting a church in America and is interviewed in front of the whole congregation. He is asked what he and his wife do back home in England when they have finished at church. Great hilarity is caused when he answers that he and his wife go home and have a joint.

When I have talked about Christ with young people, as far as they are concerned, I might as well have been talking about the man on the moon. They do not know what I mean.

These young people do not know enough about the faith even to be described as 'non- Christians'. They are at a stage before being 'non-Christians'. They are 'pre-Christians'.

People are labouring under the false impression that to talk about Christ will automatically trigger a certain reaction in a cause-and-effect equation. The truth is that in a pre-Christian society people don't know enough about Christianity to know what they think.

Methods of evangelism appropriate for a pre-Christian culture need to be developed.

How can we be so right?

TELL THE STORY

In a pre-Christian culture evangelism is not about explaining the gospel, but rather it becomes a process of telling and asking—telling the gospel story to the young people and asking what they think. It is not my job to present the gospel in what I see as being the most culturally relevant form for the young people. If I am telling rather than explaining the gospel story, then the young people will work out the relevance of Christianity for themselves.

The mistake that people make in a pre-Christian society is to feel the need to explain the story with a set of thoughts and ideas that do not mean anything to the young person listening. The lesson that I have learnt again and again over the past five years is to tell the story, and then to shut up and listen to how the young people react to what it is they have heard.

There is no more simple method of evangelism than story-telling. It is a method of evangelism that places the need for 'personal discovery' and 'working it out' (on the young people's behalf) alongside the need for 'information transmission' (on our behalf).

One young person was fascinated with the idea of God 'laying out' Paul. If I had explained to him that, in fact, God had a plan and that Paul was going to preach the gospel to the Gentiles, and so on, and so on, then he would quickly have lost interest. Who is to say that my middle-class, long-term, calculating, planning view of God is more authentic than his immediate Bermondsey street-culture understanding. All I am doing is telling the story and allowing him to work out what he thinks of what he is hearing.

I spent two years working in a pre-Christian culture in India. We had responsibility for five villages outside Madras which we were not able to visit each week. We paid a Hindu girl to read from the scriptures every Sunday at the same time. Then in the sixth week, we would come through the village at that time and find people discussing what was meant by the gospel stories. In the same way, if we don't allow young people the space to work this out for themselves, then we are weighing the excitement and interest of the gospel story with layer upon layer of boredom and obligation and duty. It is a waste of time and energy trying to second guess young people by developing work that we think will be more relevant to them. It is a question of relationships with young people and talking and listening to their answers.

Another young person in Bermondsey thought that the Good Shepherd was a 'tight git' for leaving the ninety-nine sheep to go and look for the one that was lost. Jesus was 'shitting himself' with fear in the Garden of Gethsemane, and Joseph thought that it was a 'liberty' (that is, an outrage) for Mary to be pregnant and the idea that she was pregnant by the Holy Spirit was 'macca' (Cockney rhyming slang—macaroni... pony... pony and trap... crap). As long as they are given the space to work out the implications for themselves, then young people are hungry and fascinated by the gospel stories. Working with these young people, I avoid the temptation of always trying to explain the significance of Christianity. Instead, I tell the story of Christ and ask them what they think.

I worked with one group of young people, where we started worshipping and praying within the first month of them coming into the church. If they said they did not know how to pray, I would tell them to start by talking at the ceiling and then build up towards God. This is not conventional theology; it runs the risk of presenting God as the man up in the sky; however, the central point is that it throws the responsibility for working out what was meant back on to the pre-Christian young person. When it is appropriate for us to talk in more detail about prayer it is something that the young people have already been doing and working out for themselves. With the pre-Christian young person, the power and immediacy of prayer can be throttled if you look for a concept to explain what prayer is, and then get people to start praying in line with what you think is a good concept.

In many people's minds, the idea of becoming a Christian is indistinguishable from 'making a commitment'. The idea of making a commitment does presuppose a knowledge base that will be available to a non-Christian rather than a pre-Christian. For a pre-Christian the idea of a commitment can be very conceptual—'on the basis of what you have mentally understood out of all that you have heard, are you prepared to mentally commit your life to Christ?'—it is clumsy and unnecessary. The progress to becoming a Christian is more gradual and is more likely to be a case of recognizing what has happened already in their lives, than committing themselves to what they think we think could happen in their lives.

BUILD UP A COMMON LANGUAGE

There is a need to challenge pre-Christian young people who have heard the gospel story and have come to firmly-held conclusions that are wrong and damaging, for example Christians are wimps, God is a nasty old man, and so on, and so on.

The situation is the same in that I use the word 'Jesus' and it means one thing to me and another thing to the young people. There is a need to deconstruct a lot of the preconceived ideas that the young people have about what they think words mean and then also to deconstruct what they think we as Christians think those words mean.

At times, I have deliberately set out to confuse. On one occasion at a weekend camp, a leader was unable to sleep because there was so much noise. He got up at three in the morning and started a water fight. On another occasion in the minibus people are singing. I shout 'make some noise' at the top of my voice until after twenty minutes all of us are hoarse with exhaustion. This might break every textbook definition of youthwork, but we are creating a controlled confusion that will lead on to the young people asking questions, which will lead on to discussions about Christ and Christianity. The need, then, is to build up a common language with the young people.

I have led discussions around many of the basic emotions in order to establish a common currency about what words mean. On one occasion, someone read a letter telling them that a relationship had finished; a discussion ensued about getting hurt; after twenty minutes an understanding was established and there was a word that could be used, without any fear of being misunderstood, when talking about Jesus.

On another occasion, there was a piece of drama about a guy who lends his tape recorder to a friend. The friend loses it. The guy gets very annoyed but grudgingly says that he will forgive him. The friend who lost the tape recorder disappears. Someone else comes round the corner and the guy slags his friend off for losing the tape recorder. A discussion ensued about what is meant by forgiveness and a common understanding was formed. Often young people have had a far more profound understanding of forgiveness than Christians.

The style of teaching that is appropriate for the pre-Christian young person is that of 'primary pictures'. This means teaching that does not need any explanation, but leaves the listener to make the connections and to work it out for themselves. I consciously shake off the laborious sketch and explanation method, where someone does a piece of drama and someone else appears and asks people if they knew what the drama meant. All that has happened with this method of teaching is that the young people mimic our thought structure rather than adopt their own.

The apocryphal story of the school assembly makes this point. The person taking the assembly is telling the young people how she was sitting in her front room and saw a furry animal with a bushy tail sitting up a tree eating some nuts. What did they think that it was? One of the young people replies that although it sounds like a squirrel, the answer must be Jesus—'Can we go now?'

I once read a story from *Winnie-the-Pooh* and then a story about someone being wrongfully arrested and put on trial. I asked the young people which was the true story, and when they replied it was the story about the man being arrested, I told them it was from the Bible. It is a question of having a strong enough nerve to leave it at that. So many Christians are frightened and feel that if they don't get the name of Jesus in full square smack in the young person's face, then they are not doing their job. This is both clumsy and ineffective evangelism.

On another occasion, we put on an enormous feast at the local church. We got everyone to chip in £5 or £10 and we spent £200 on turkey and chicken and ham and crisps. We had enough food for 150 people to walk out of the church with their bellies full and we still had enough left to give some to the homeless people living in Lincoln's Inn Field. When we were getting the food ready, the young people were for ever stuffing sandwiches into their pockets; when we had the feast, they sat there looking at all the food in amazement. If they couldn't work out that the food was being offered to them free and that no one was going to shout at them for taking too much, then what chance have they got of realizing that eternal life is being offered to them by God?

When I took out a group to do some shopping for the feast, they could not believe that we had £50 to spend and they could get whatever they wanted. They kept on wanting to try and steal things and I kept on telling them that there was no need and that we could buy it. The trip to the supermarket is an acted out parable of the love of God. If young people can't work out that if they want a bar of white milk chocolate then they can have it by right and do not have to steal it, then what chance do they have of working out that eternal life is also theirs by right?

A different group of younger people were fascinated by an exercise where rather than looking for a concept to explain what is meant by forgiveness of sins, I got them to write on pieces of paper what they felt bad about. We put all of these pieces of paper into a large bin and then we burnt them. They were getting more and more of their friends to come and do this exercise with them and we were in danger of setting off the fire alarms. This piece of work culminated in a Christmas party, again with food and drink and music. Thirty young people burnt pieces of paper and thereby understood what Jesus had done for them without a word being spoken.

AND DON'T FORGET THE CHURCH

What the church is suffering from is a fundamental loss of nerve.

⊙ When a herd of animals is reduced in numbers, all the animals will run around twice as fast kicking up a lot of dust. The purpose of this is to generate a feeling of security.

⊙ When Christians are asked to explain the salvation message to a young person they will complicate the message because they are so painfully worried about what the young person is going to do. Subliminally, a lot of the time, Christians are not saying, 'Hear the powerful and exciting news of Jesus Christ.' Instead they are saying, 'Become like us... make us feel more secure... guard us in our insecurities.'

The mistake that Christians are making when they do this is that they are confusing sanctification with redemption. Sanctification is something very difficult and demanding, and needs to be worked out with fear and trembling. Redemption is something basic and straightforward, and needs to be described as such. Ask a group of people what

2+2 is and they will look at you suspiciously wondering why you have asked the question—'What does he want?', 'Does he mean 22?' The answer is that $2+2=4$; Margaret Thatcher is an English woman, Naples is in Italy and Christ died for our sins. Sanctification and life-choices are complicated; redemption is not.

The reality of a pre-Christian culture presents a great opportunity to the church in the 1990s to ensure that young people do get to hear the gospel story. What I have found is that if in telling the gospel story I keep what I am saying simple and I don't shroud it round with long explanations, then I am constantly surprised at how fascinated young people are to hear what it is that I have to say. People become Christians and God's name is glorified.

5

Growth or dependency: polarities of youthwork practice

PETER BALL

Casting the 'proverbial eye' across the spectrum of youthwork practice in evidence today it is clear that the issues of growth and dependency are still paramount. Whether our work with young people is couched in terms of a directive or non-directive style, participative or non-participative approaches, or authoritarian or democratic leadership, the extent to which we enable young people to grow away from their dependence upon us, and others, will influence their ability to function ultimately as mature adults, as well as their ability to adopt independent patterns of living. For Christian youthworkers, of course, there is the added dimension of the young people's growth towards maturity in the Christian faith, and we will be concerned to facilitate their ongoing spiritual development through the programmes we offer and the relationships we gradually build with them. If our concern, too, is truly for their development in a holistic sense, for their growth as 'whole-beings', then we must also be encouraging them to engage with all facets of their life—work, play, body, mind, culture, relationships—holding all of this together firmly in a Christian context.

Youthworkers, irrespective of their preferred style of leadership and degree of commitment to the participation of young people in the decision-making processes of their group or organization, irrespective of their effectiveness in bringing young people to a greater sense of self-awareness, and irrespective of the extent to which they are able to increase the young people's understanding of God and their growth as young Christians, will recognize the fact that in establishing contact with young people and seeking to communicate with them, an immediate dependence is established. The intervention is most likely to have been initiated by the worker and not by the young person. We are most likely to be intervening on our terms and not those of the young people we are working with. Therefore, the nature of that initial contact, and of the way in which the relationship between worker and young person develops will have a direct bearing on the degree of dependency which might be established. In very simple terms, if the youthworker's response to a young person is directive or judgmental, leaving little scope for negotiation or compromise, or if the 'activity' options on offer to the young person are predetermined by the youthworker with little or no consultation with the young person, the nature of the relationship will be quite different from that which develops from a situation in which the young person's opinion is always sought, and his or her decisions are honoured and acted upon. Moving young people on from any sense of dependence which exists in the relationship between them and the youthworker is vital if our aim of bringing them to maturity as young Christians is going to be achieved.

It is anticipated that this chapter will raise more questions than provide answers. In fact it begins with a series of questions for youthwork practitioners that have arisen throughout its preparation and from conversations with youthworkers themselves:

⊙ To what extent do, or can, youthworkers 'allow' participation in youthwork on terms determined by the young people they are seeking to serve?

⊙ To what extent are the aims of the youthworker, and the agency for whom she/he is working, synonymous with the expectations of young people?

⊙ To what extent are youthworkers prepared to relinquish power and control?

⊙ To what extent are youthworkers conscious of the inherent dependency which exists in their relationships with young people?

It is hoped that this chapter will promote some ongoing discussion around the issues of growth and dependency, some consideration of youthwork practice in the area of participation and empowerment of young people, and some further understanding of the nature of our growth towards Christian maturity.

Why elect to focus on the questions of growth or dependency? A great deal of work with young adults in youth services in the United Kingdom, including youthwork undertaken in a Christian context, has been shaped by a notion of a 'participative' approach. Such approaches have encouraged young people:

⊙ to take responsibility for their own actions

⊙ to develop decision-making skills

⊙ to take responsibility for the design and delivery of certain aspects of the programme or curriculum

⊙ to become involved in policy-making through representation on 'management' or 'church' committees

In the early days of such initiatives within youth organizations this often manifested itself in the form of 'members committees' or 'councils', and/or representation on the adult boards and councils of their respective organizations. Such developments serve as good vehicles for training young people in 'committee procedure', for giving them a good understanding of the formal structures and roles within the management of their 'parent' body or organization. For some young adults who have a propensity towards responding to this style of participative youthwork, such opportunities have been, and can be, very successful in equipping them for similar roles and responsibilities in many different facets of their future adult lives.

However, it is becoming increasingly difficult for a growing proportion of young adults to engage in a participative style focusing upon structures and cultures which are beyond their experience. As a consequence, opportunities for young people to take personal responsibility within their youth organizations may be increasingly focused upon short-term commitments, often issue-based, but still enabling them to develop decision-making skills and to take responsibility for their own actions. Certainly, many young people have gained, and will continue to gain, a tremendous amount from such experiences—but many will not be able to engage with this type of process at all.

'Participation' continues to be a key focus amongst youthworkers and within youth organizations in the United Kingdom. The adoption of a 'participative approach' and 'young people's participation in decision-making processes' continue to be elements of youthwork practice expected by our political masters and funders, as well as gaining prominence in many job descriptions for youthwork appointments. With the continuing recognition of a youth service curriculum, with the advent of service agreements between 'funders' and 'providers' (whether central or local government, or other agencies), and with the growing demand for practitioners (even within the church) to be more accountable for their work, the ways in which we empower young people to function more effectively within our organizations, and also the ways in which we empower them to take control of their own lives, will come under increasing degrees of scrutiny.

For many youth organizations there may be a long tradition of, and continuing strong focus on, young people's participation in their decision-making processes and structures—this is valid and appropriate for those young people who can engage with such predominantly 'adult' ways of doing things.

In fact, such participation can be most helpful in preparing for fuller adult involvement and leadership roles within our youth organizations as well as the wider community. However, as already stated, for those young people who find such involvement difficult there is a need to make participation more accessible. We need to recognize their need for preparation, training and support, and offer opportunities for this. We need to recognize that young people will see through anything which is merely tokenism. We need to recognize that overt positive discrimination towards young adults may be necessary in the early stages of any empowerment process, particularly a process in which they are going to encounter a culture and structure of which they have little, or no, experience.

Participation in practice

If the hope, in encouraging young people to participate at all levels (national, regional and local) of the church's structures and decision-making processes, is that young people will have more power and influence, then can we, initially, leave their representation to chance? The real likelihood of young adults finding themselves naturally appointed or elected to representative roles might be quite rare; and the few young people who might manage to find their way into a representative role would be hard-pressed to sustain themselves through the subsequent process without adequate support, encouragement and training.

Many of the major denominations have taken steps to ensure that the voice of young people is heard within their decision-making structures; that young people have a representative voice. Some would say that the steps we have taken are small ones—and, yes, we certainly have a long way to travel along the road of empowering young people to take up their rightful place in the decision-making processes of the church. What is worth noting is that, as more and more young people are given opportunities to participate, they grow in their personal self-esteem and confidence, and acquire an increased determination to be heard!

This 'cameo' of young adult participation may well be symbolic of much of our 'participation' and 'empowerment' work with young people. Yes, it is important that we seek to involve them in these procedures, structures and decision-making processes. And, yes, many young people benefit from these experiences by learning new skills and developing their God-given gifts—some perhaps showing potential for future leadership roles, and being offered appropriate training and support to achieve leadership status.

However, we are left with some serious questions about a focus on empowerment and participation which may, actually, be meeting the organization's needs more readily than the personal development needs of young people. Questions come to mind such as:

⊙ How much of this is about engaging with issues young people are facing in their daily lives?

⊙ How much of this is about encouraging young people's growth towards independence?

⊙ How much of this is about the nurture of young people as Christians?

⊙ How much of this is about sustaining a dependent relationship with adults and about sustaining adult control of the existing structures rather than the empowerment of young people?

Furthermore:

⊙ How prepared are we to give young people experience of participation on their own terms?

⊙ How independent are we prepared to allow (sorry, enable) young people to become?

⊙ How risky are we prepared to be in empowering young people? And, finally:

⊙ What might the consequences of giving young people independence and power be?

Signs of growing Christian maturity during adolescence

As Christian youthworkers one of our prime tasks must be to lead young people towards mature, Christian, adulthood. We have a concern for the development of young people as 'whole' persons; their physical, mental, spiritual and social development. Part of that responsibility involves, as has already been discussed, providing opportunities for young people to function and participate within the church or youth group 'structures' of which they are part and through which their voices need to be heard. Another part of that responsibility concerns their development as young Christians. Looking now at what signs of Christian maturity we might hope to see in young people, we may be provided with some other indicators of how young people might be helped to grow towards independence, to grow 'out of' dependency.

When we are building relationships with young people and helping them to grow in their faith what signs of Christian maturity might we be looking for? What might help us begin to understand more about the process that we, and our young people, are engaging in? Charles M. Shelton, in his book *Adolescent Spirituality*,[1] offers us some signs of Christian maturity to focus upon which include our:

- Christ-centredness;

- Christian commitment;

- approach to prayer;

- focus on others;

- openness;

- acceptance.

I would like to consider each of these in turn.

CHRIST-CENTREDNESS

The fact that adolescence is a time of questioning, self-doubt and searching for meaning in life makes the path towards Christian maturity a rocky and uneven one for many young people. Periods of doubt and questioning can draw them away from God, so it will not be surprising to discover that young people's understanding and experience of him fluctuates markedly. However, it is not uncommon for young people to:

- recognize the person of Jesus as someone to confide in;

- let Jesus' principles of living guide their moral decisions and choices;

⊙ gain a greater understanding of Jesus' calling for them as individuals.

For many young people embarking on their Christian pilgrimage the question 'How does Jesus make a difference in my life?' is often a constant and crucial one. As youthworkers we have a responsibility to help young people explore this question for themselves.

CHRISTIAN COMMITMENT

Adolescents are often searching for their 'true' identity and frequently seeking an answer to the question 'What is the purpose of my life—what direction is it taking?' They experience the tensions inherent in formulating a value system which they can honour and own for themselves. The Christian youthworker's responsibility lies in offering the gospel to young people in a way that deepens their understanding of it, and in a way that enables them to begin to own and develop a Christian value system.

This will lead young people to accept, more readily, responsibility for their own actions. It will lead them to a stronger appreciation of others for who, and what, they are.

APPROACH TO PRAYER

Creating opportunities for young people to be open to Jesus in a prayerful way will enable them to find security in him and to discover their innate capacity to share their deepest joys and sorrows with him. Focusing on prayer will provide a means of supporting and sustaining their Christian values in what has become a predominantly secular world. Focusing on prayer will enable young people to listen more to Jesus, ponder on what they hear him saying to them, and begin to discern where he is leading them.

FOCUS ON OTHERS

In becoming more Christ-centred, in developing a stronger

Christian commitment, and through experience of prayer, young people come to accept themselves 'as they are', and come to understand more and more that God's love for them (us) is unconditional. This acceptance of self, a valuing of the self, enables young people to move away from the 'self-centredness' so often attributed to adolescents; they are more able to focus on the needs and concerns of others. Their growing experience of Jesus leads them to appreciate others more.

OPENNESS

Not only will young people come to accept and value themselves more, they will also come to trust themselves more. In gaining this trust in themselves they are able to venture into new experiences, and encounter new people and new situations, with growing confidence. This will contribute enormously to their exploration of their own lives and lifestyles, and enable them to be more reflective.

ACCEPTANCE

Through experience of 'self-affirming' encounters with others any 'critique' of young people as individuals may become easier for them to cope with and may well, in fact, lead to a realization of their personal limitations and weaknesses... and, perhaps, their faults. Knowing and accepting our faults, the things we do wrong, the ways in which we fall short or 'miss the mark', bring a deeper understanding of the need for repentance and reconciliation. Feelings of guilt become a sign to us that we have 'lost our way'.

This journey through a process leading towards Christian maturity brings into sharp focus, again, the need for the developing relationship between youthworker and young person to be established in such a way as to allow freedom for growth. None of us can make another person's 'journey' or prepare them for the path along which they are going to travel. In his recent publication, *Further Along the Road Less Travelled*, M. Scott Peck reflects upon the parable of the ten virgins waiting for Christ, or God, to appear. You will recall that five of the virgins prepared their lamps with oil in readiness should this appearance occur at night. The other five had not taken such steps and were not prepared at all for the eventual night-time appearance. The virgins who had been waiting in readiness refused to share their oil with the others. Now, one might have expected God to chastise them for such an uncharitable, uncaring reaction, but what he did, in effect, was to praise the wise virgins for their actions in being prepared. Thinking this through, Scott Peck came to realize that the oil was symbolic of our preparation, and that what Jesus was saying to us was that we cannot share our preparation; we cannot prepare for others. The only thing we can do is to do our utmost to motivate and encourage others to prepare for themselves. And this most definitely includes our young people.

This chapter will, hopefully, stimulate some discussion and reflection around the issues of growth and dependency in the relationship between youthworker and young person. In addition, it is hoped that consideration will be given to ways in which we help young people to grow to maturity as Christians and involve them in a participative way in our churches.

If you have had the opportunity to visit the Taizé community in France and witness the thousands of young people who flock there each summer, you will have been encouraged by their eagerness in searching for truth and meaning in their lives. This community welcomes young people 'unconditionally', accepting them 'just as they are', and a final contribution to this chapter must be from Brother Roger, the founder of that community. He said:

I would go to the uttermost ends of the earth, to the world's farthest end, to tell that I trust the new generations, that I trust the young! We who are older must listen and never condemn. Listen, always listen, and so grasp the very best of the creative intuitions alive in today's youth.

Brother Roger went on to say:

The young are going to open up paths, break down walls, overturn obstacles in their path and draw the whole people of God forward in their train.

And finally:

Personally, from my youth onwards I had the conviction that to be really human the main thing was never to condemn anybody, but first to understand everything about each person.

Many youthworkers will identify strongly with what Brother Roger said. My prayer is that our churches will make such a declaration to our young people, that they will trust and listen to our young people more and more, that we all will support our young people in their quest for truth and greater understanding of God in their lives.

NOTES

1. Charles M. Shelton, *Adolescent Spirituality*, Loyola University Press, 1983.

6

Programme and relationships in youth ministry

CHRISTINE COOK

Introduction

In recent years, many people on the Continent, and more specifically in French-speaking Europe, have become aware of a growing need for training in the area of adolescent, or youth, ministry. This need has long been recognized in Great Britain and in the United States, but unfortunately, until recently, it has been ignored on the Continent. In the past few years, both myself and two counterparts of mine, one in Belgium working with 'Jeunesse et Vie' and the other in France working with 'Jeunesse Ardente', have been asked by local Bible Institutes to offer an elective course in youth ministry for their students.

This demand for training denotes a growing realization of the fact that young people in French-speaking Europe today make up a very special category of the population and that the traditional means of evangelism, or even of Christian education, are no longer as valid or as reliable as they used to be. Christian organizations, Bible Institutes, pastors and parents are all seeking to understand the youth of their country, and are trying to find efficient ways of reaching them. They are looking to specialists to help in this understanding, and to train both lay people and pastors in youth ministry.

The question which then arises is: What kind of training? What is most needed in reaching young people today? Historically, when a church, a youth organization or an individual wanted to reach young people or children, they set up some meetings and invited the youngsters to attend. If the programme was interesting enough, young people would come and perhaps even bring their friends. Today, a deeper understanding is needed to reach a very complex generation. Programmes, as such, no longer seem to be sufficient either to keep young people in a church or to reach those outside the church. So what is needed?

It was basically this question, What kind of training?, which prompted me to design a research project. This project came under the auspices of a Masters Degree which I was working on at the University of Geneva. The aim of the research was to discover how youthworkers saw their role and compare those results with how young people saw the role or function of a youth leader. The results, I hoped, would shed some light on the question of training and, more importantly, on the basic issue of what is needed in youth ministry: programme or relationships. Much of this chapter will be reflections from that Masters thesis.

In French-speaking Europe, there is no opportunity to be trained as a professional Christian youthworker. The profession simple doesn't exist. State-trained youthworkers come under three main categories: 'animateur' (youth leader), 'educateur' (social worker) and 'educateur spécialisé' (social worker for the handicapped or socially deviant). The category which comes closest to a Christian youthworker is the category of 'animateur'. It was around this category of person that the research project was built.

The French-speaking perspective

The first step was to understand the specificity of a youthworker. The specific title given to the kind of youthworker which comes closest to a British or American youth pastor is an 'animateur socio-culturel'. Geneviève Pujol puts it this way, 'This person is different from a teacher or another youthworker in the emphasis s/he puts on interpersonal relationships and personal contacts. Indeed, relationships become more important than a learning process or the transmission of information.'[1]

Michel Simonot, a well-known French author in the area of 'animation', defines this kind of youthwork as follows: 'Socio-cultural youthwork is a section of social life whose workers have dedicated themselves to the goal of bringing about a kind of transformation of attitudes and collective as well as inter-individual relationships by means of direct action on those individuals, their attitudes, their inter-individual and social relationships. This action is carried on usually through different activities using a non-directive or active methodology.'[2]

It is interesting to note that non-Christian professional youthworkers are defining themselves in terms of relationships. However, they see these relationships being worked out through different activities, that is organized activities. Many French and Swiss 'animateurs socio-culturels' work in a youth centre which offers different workshops (guitar lessons, theatre, arts and crafts) or outings during school holidays. The framework for developing relationships is within an organized programme.

The next step was to take a look at adolescents themselves. What are their needs? What are they looking for in the way of relationships? Young people over the years have progressively occupied a more and more dominant place in society. For centuries, they lived in a situation of almost total dependency on adults. Today, they are very much detached from adult influence. One very marked difference between the 1960s and the 1990s is what constitutes the frame of reference for young people. In the 1960s, family and school were the main sources of influence for young people. In the 1990s, those two systems have been replaced by the media and peers.

With the breakdown of the family unit and an overall rejection of adult forms of authority, young people turn to friends as a main source of relationships. During adolescence, young people are in the process of defining who they are, independently of their family and parents. Ideally, this process should be able to take place not only with peers but also in dialogue with parents and other adults close to the young person. Unfortunately, this process is now taking place for the most part solely with other adolescents who are in the same process of self-definition, and, therefore, not able to step back and get a better perspective on the whole definition process.

Young people like to get together with each other no matter what activity is offered or practised. For them, the essential element is spending a couple of hours together with peers, to be able to say what they like, think what they like, experience and discover what they like, together with others in an atmosphere in which they feel at ease.

Edouard Limbos, another recognized French author, says this in his book on training in human sciences: 'The motivations pushing young people to get together in a group are variable. The dominant factors influencing adolescents are one, to escape from family constraints and to be free to experience different activities in a mixed group, two, to find an agreeable atmosphere where one can freely discuss and express oneself, and three, to participate in different activities with friends.'[3]

Young people in Geneva, Switzerland, once they leave ninth grade (end of mandatory education), are spread out all over the city according to what type of training they are pursuing, that is apprenticeships, general education, business education, classical education. Others drop out of the educational process altogether and either get a job, travel or go on unemployment. They are no longer linked by the geography of where they live. Relationships with groups of friends are formed through many channels. Some people will belong to a certain group of friends and have to travel forty minutes on public transportation to get together. This, however, is not at all seen as a hindrance to their getting together and spending time with one another.

Young people hold the group in very high esteem. During adolescence, they are very often in conflict with their family and with adults in general as it is they who represent the authority structure of society. They find a kind of release or outlet in groups of their peers, as well as the possibility of building emotional ties with others, which is absolutely essential to their well-being and development.

Young people do not gather in groups to learn a skill or to receive a message. Nor are these groups just organized for leisure time. They find their purpose in a social, psychological and moral finality. The gathering has meaning because of the individuals present, because of their actions and thoughts, their relationships and their joint consciousness.

In another work entitled 'Animation of cultural and leisure-time groups', Edouard Limbos explains what he considers to be the finality of socio-cultural groups. Such groups aim 'to allow each individual to discover her/himself, to participate in the life of the group and the society by proposing changes, improvements and a permanent increase in the quality of life; to favour the endorsement of goals freely elaborated within the group according to the needs, aspirations and problems experienced by each person; to experience relationships with others while respecting each individual, her/his values, beliefs and social background; and to allow each person to find her/his place freely by living in accordance with her/his own frame of reference.'[4]

The group is an important element in the life of a young person. There will be a collective consciousness that allows a group to exist and that allows its members to be attached to the group, whether they are physically present or momentarily separated from the group.

What role can a youthworker play in this type of situation? He or she must first of all be accepted by the young people getting together. Very often this will happen through a shared experience, a crisis or simply by the youthworker celebrating and enjoying who the young people are. The youthworker, in this setting, hopes to help the adolescents present learn how to use their freedom, to find personal well-being and growth, and to adapt themselves to the social and community life around them. The essential element in such a group is not activity as such (the materials nor the ingenuity of the methods used), but rather the degree of personal conviction the youth leader possesses about the young person, as well as a sense of imagination and a spirit of initiative that she or he can put forth without diminishing the creativity of the group.

When a more organized activity is called for, the role of the youthworker is to allow every young person to feel at ease, experience joy and be understood. He or she is at the service of every participant, to help everyone to understand better who they are and where they have come from, in order to help them better define what they want to become. In this perspective, every young person can discover for themselves what makes up their originality as well as their aspirations.

Youthworkers will be effective much more because of who they are than because of what they do or the techniques they possess. Much more than a question of method or material, good youthwork is a matter of human quality. Jean Leveugle puts it this way: 'To possess an interior wealth, to want not only to share it but mostly to incite others to build their own personal qualities, such is the first and fundamental condition of all good youthwork.'[5]

It was with these convictions and this background that we started on the research which would help confirm the hypothesis with which we started out, namely that in order to reach young people today, the basic model that needs to be explored and developed is a relational one rather than one based on a programme. In order to define the type of training that is necessary for youthworkers, it is first of all necessary to know what the final product should look like.

Research project

Forty-five youthworkers from Switzerland, France and Belgium were asked to classify forty-two different characteristics of youthworkers from the most to the least important. The majority of these characteristics were gleaned from a pre-research document in which youthworkers were asked to describe freely the ideal youthworker. The persons participating in the research were both male and female, aged from nineteen to forty-six years, with between one and twenty-eight years of experience in different kinds of youthwork. All were in one way or another related to an organization either Christian or state-run.

Out of the forty-two characteristics, eleven could be said to enhance the development of relationships between young people and others in the group, twenty-four had more to do with skills or personality, and seven could be considered to hinder the development of relationships as they denote a youthworker who is more or less centred on her/himself instead of on the young person or on the group dynamics.

Research results

The following are the characteristics which showed up as the most important in an overall classification of the forty-five participants put together:

⊙ being able to listen;

⊙ being authentic;

⊙ knowing how to work in a team;

⊙ respecting the personality of the young person;

⊙ caring about others;

⊙ having time to devote to young people; and

⊙ having worked out one's own identity.

The results were further classified by sex, age, years of experience and nationality. These results were, however, very similar and any difference was so minor as not to be worth mentioning. None of the differences were significant statistically. It seems as though there is a strong consensus on the part of youthworkers regardless of their age, their sex, their years of experience and their nationality as to what an ideal youthworker should be like. Although a large percentage of those participating in this research were working in a Christian setting, there was no major difference between their results and those turned in by non-Christian employed youthworkers.

It is further interesting to note that out of the seven leading characteristics chosen by all the youthworkers put together, the first five have to do with relational qualities (being able to listen, being authentic, knowing how to work in a team, respecting the personality of the young person, caring about others). From this observation, it is clear that there is a consensus among youthworkers in French-speaking Europe that the ideal youthworker is one who is developing relational skills rather than programme skills. None of the programme skills were ranked very highly at all. This observation seems to be true regardless of the age, sex, years of experience or nationality of the youthworker.

The next part of the research was to give the same list of forty-two characteristics of youthworkers to eighty adolescents ranging in age from thirteen to twenty years of age. They were asked to do the same thing as the youthworkers, that is to classify the forty-two characteristics according to their importance in defining an ideal youthworker.

The following are the characteristics which showed up as the most important in an overall classification of all eighty adolescents put together:

⊙ being dynamic;

⊙ being able to listen;

⊙ respecting the personality of the young person;

⊙ having time to devote to young people;

⊙ knowing how to talk to young people;

⊙ knowing how to give confidence to a young person;

⊙ having a good sense of humour; and

⊙ being enthusiastic.

In contrast to the youthworkers participating in the research, the adolescents did not choose systematically only those characteristics which enhance the relational aspect of youthwork. Out of the eight items they chose as most important, four had to do with relational qualities and four with personality traits. The conclusion that we drew from this is that adolescents value the personality of a youthworker as much as her/his relational qualities. They see both as equally important and as an ensemble.

This tends to confirm the fact that young people are more concerned with the person of a youthworker than the skills or capacities that s/he represents. Much more than a matter of material or methodology, good youthwork has to do with the nature of the youthworker and her/his relational skills.

It is not surprising that young people are looking at the personality of the youthworker, rather than seeing his or her relational skills at work. Since they are still in the process of forming their own identity, they are not always capable of taking a step back, and getting a perspective on who they are and why they relate in such or such a way. What strikes the young person first of all is the personality of the youthworker, and the fact that s/he is being listened to and cared for.

Minor differences did exist between the different classifications by the young people according to sex or age, but they are not statistically significant and therefore it is not worth going into any detail on them. Suffice it to say that a consensus of opinion concerning the ideal profile of a youthworker was apparent among the eighty adolescents tested.

Conclusions

In French-speaking countries, the profession of youth-worker in community, state-run or private institutions has developed only since the 1970s. What used to be considered a pastime or hobby for young adults is taking on a more and more widely recognized place in the professional world. The needs of adolescents, modern sociology and the increasing amount of leisure time all mean that there is a growing urgency for qualified professionals to provide care for young people. When we speak about qualifications, we must speak about training. In order to have professional youthworkers, they must be trained and we believe that the results of this research can provide some avenues of reflection as to the kind of training that is necessary.

The results of our research show that the main goal of the youthworker is to establish relationships with young people. Indeed, it is because of a solid relationship established between youthworkers and young people that the latter can define themselves and find a balance in their lives. The programme aspect of youthwork is there to provide a means to access this relationship. Research results show that it is more important for youthworkers to take courses which develop interpersonal relational skills, help them to better understand their own personal dynamics and history, rather than activity or programme techniques.

As mentioned earlier, almost all youthwork done in Geneva is carried out as an organized activity. Contact-Jeunes, the organization for which I work, is perhaps the only one which encourages its staff just to spend time building relationships with teenagers, wherever they may be. We have found, nevertheless, that adolescents do like to have something they can 'come to' which is fun and attractive for them. They will only come with their friends or if their friends are coming, however.

The youth leaders must be dynamic, have a good sense of humour and be enthusiastic for the adolescents even to want to be associated with them. However, it is essential for youth leaders to remember that what young people are really searching for is to be heard, to be understood and to be respected. They must use both their enthusiastic personality and a dynamic programme as a means to enter into a meaningful relationship with adolescents only.

Therefore, when thinking of setting up a training programme for youth leaders, it is essential to put a lot of emphasis on the basic character traits of the person undergoing training, on the development of her or his interpersonal, relational skills and lastly on certain programme techniques. Unfortunately, it is much easier to learn certain programme techniques than to spend the major part of one's time listening to adolescents and developing quality relationships with them. It is much easier to train someone in programme techniques than to help her/him to develop and work on her/his own personal relationships. It is sometimes even easier to offer a large and intricate programme, instead of opening oneself up to a young person. And yet this study shows that most youthworkers and major authors agree that the main goal of youthwork is centred around relationships.

If this is true in a non-Christian study on youthwork and youthworkers, how much more important is it for Christians to realize the basic need for building relationships? I would say that Bible teaching and catechism are important 'programme' items to say nothing of meetings and camps for young people. The ministry in which I am involved in Switzerland has weekly meetings and an active camping programme. Yet those are only the visible items of our ministry. The major part of our ministry takes place in individual encounters, at school, in homes and in pubs, being with young people in their environment and on their terms. Therefore, on the basis of this research and my own personal experience, I would strongly say that the most effective means of reaching young people and helping them, in turn, meet Jesus Christ is not by what we do as youthworkers, not by the kind of programme we present, but by who we are and by the quality of the relationships we can develop with them.

NOTES

1. Geneviève Poujol, *Profession: animateur*, ed. Edouard Privat, 1989.

2. Michel Simonot, *Les animateurs socioculturels*, PUF, 1974.

3. Edouard Limbos, *La formation des animateurs de groupes de jeunes, formation permanente en sciences humaines*, ed. ESF, 1979.

4. Edouard Limbos, *L'animation des groupes de culture et de loisir*, ed. ESF, 1984.

5. Jean Leveugle, *Devenir animateur et savoir animer, comment former et se former pour pratiquer l'animation*, ed. Edouard Privat, 1977.

7

Emerging patterns of youth ministry at the end of the twentieth century

MARK H. SENTER III

Tony was an articulate African-American in his early twenties. As I listened to him talk with fellow youth ministry types around a dinner table, I concluded that Tony was the prototype of a hustler. His 'hustle', however, was not drugs or sex. It was Christ. His turf was inner-city Indianapolis, Indiana—though the twelfth largest city in the United States, not known for crime and poverty, yet struggling with the crumbling social system common to most cities of the world.

His ideas did not appear to reflect the programme strategy commonly associated with his organization. Out of curiosity I asked, 'How long do you think you will stay with this youth ministry organization?' He appeared shocked that I would ask. His charisma had positioned him as one of the darlings of the conference.

After checking out my motives for asking, Tony candidly replied, 'Maybe another year.' Now it was my time to be shocked. 'Why so soon?' I asked, marvelling more at the speed than the fact of his departure. 'They make me do clubs,' was Tony's straightforward reply.

'And what is wrong with clubs?' I inquired. After all parachurch youth ministry had been synonymous with club meetings since the 1940s and church-based youth fellowships/societies since the 1880s.

'My guys think all these games we are supposed to do are a bunch of crap. They are ideas dreamed up by some honkey out in the 'burbs to keep bored rich kids happy.'[1]

'So what is your alternative?' I asked.

'Job training!' he shot back without blinking an eye. 'But not the kind we get in schools. The kind of training my guys need is in how to be entrepreneurs. Most of the people in the 'hood have no idea of how to gain access to the money necessary to become owners of small businesses. Other ethnic groups have their systems. African-Americans don't. We don't need games. We need careers.'

'But how would that be Christian ministry?' I asked and then wished I hadn't.

'How are a bunch of dumb games considered Christian ministry?'

Tony was right. Clubs, games, evangelistic rallies, camps, Christian schools and even youth centres are merely delivery systems for communicating the love and changing power of Jesus Christ. The fact that youthworkers are now comfortable with a certain set of approaches to reaching and discipling young people for Christ is not an adequate reason to perpetuate a given set of methodologies.

It would have been every bit as possible for Tony to earn the right to be heard by his urban friends through an entrepreneur training programme and then, in an appropriate time and in an appropriate manner, to communicate biblical truth to his friends seeking a commitment to Jesus Christ, as it was possible for Jim

Rayburn, founder of Young Life, to use a club in Gains\
Texas in 1938.

Seldom, if ever, are innovations in youth ministry complete breaks with the way effective ministries have been made in the past. On the contrary, most are a mere repackaging of methods and a refocusing on an intended audience. The subtlety of this idea may cause frustrated youthworkers to reject very useful ministry tools while seeking novelty and creativity. The genius of an entrepreneur is the ability to shift low productive energies into highly productive efforts.

Delivery systems

Youth ministry is the building of discipleship systems. When a person is working with one person at a time, little formal structure is needed because the discipler can revise and adjust the teaching/learning process at any time. The relationship resembles a conversation more than a lecture.

Once a youthworker begins ministering to groups of adolescents, structure becomes necessary. This structure or *delivery system* enables the leader to follow the words of the apostle Paul when he told Timothy, 'the things you have heard me say in the presence of many witnesses entrust to reliable men who will also be qualified to teach others' (2 Timothy 2:2).

A very important question to consider when looking for emerging patterns in youth ministry is: *What constitutes a youth ministry delivery system?* As patterns appear there is a tendency for innovators to lock onto one component of the delivery system and proclaim boldly that it is the hoped for change.

Perhaps the most frequently heard cry is for genuine relationships in which to communicate truth. Incarnational theology has served as the foundation stone of effective youth ministry for nearly two centuries though the concept was only identified by Young Life leaders in the 1940s. But strong adult-adolescent relationships, apart from a more comprehensive discipleship delivery system, will merely exhaust even the most spiritually motivated youthworker.

There are four components to such a delivery system (contact, attract, confront and train/retain). These are placed along two axes (programmatic and relational). The roles within this delivery system are shown in the diagram below.

RELATIONAL AXIS

Along the relational axis (see diagram on page 109) are two functions—contact and confront. Youth ministry begins when a Christian adult finds a comfortable way to enter the world of an adolescent. Contact is established in a meaningful manner. Conversations are enjoyed. Experiences are shared. A niche is discovered in each other's world.

Contact may be established in many ways. Natural contact happens when a Christian adult builds a friendship with a student while at work, in their neighbourhood or through

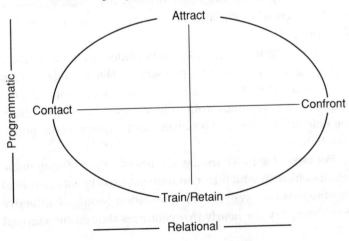

Delivery System in Youth Ministry

Relational Axis

CONTACT  CONFRONT

mutual interests. Adult-initiated contact takes place when a youthworker finds a way to share activities which the student enjoys. Programme-initiated contact happens when a church or parachurch agency sponsors an activity which is attractive to students and which is understood to require an adult presence. Parental contact happens when the relationship between young person and parent is based on trust and respect. This contact can be extended to a circle of the adolescent's friends. Issue/need-driven contact results from mutual concern over something which threatens the security of the young person's world (drugs, alcohol, violence).

Confrontation with the Christian gospel is the other end of the axis. God's truth related to God's holiness, human sinfulness and Christ's provision for salvation must be explained to the student in a manner in which the message is understood and acted upon. In a post-modern world, the importance of presenting the good news in a multi-dimensional manner is essential. Telling is no longer enough. Showing, demonstrating, experiencing as well as explaining are all part of the post-modern confrontation with the gospel.

The gospel confrontation is like drama. While the mime can communicate emotions and a general story-line, the spoken word needs to be used to provide sharp definition to a story-line. When people share a Christian worldview, the mime's presentation might be adequate. Incarnational theology might shout Christian redemption. But in a post-modern world the confrontation must be explicit and clearly defined.

Personalized Ministry

CONTACT  **CONFRONT**

The more intimate the relationship between adult and youth, the narrower the gap between contact and confrontation. But the more people who are involved in the delivery system, the more structure will be required. Spontaneity will have to be carefully planned.

PROGRAMMATIC AXIS

Along the programmatic axis (see diagram on page 111) are two functions—attracting and retaining/training. Programmes are merely delivery systems whereby groups of people can be brought with comfort and integrity to experience the Christian gospel and continue growing in a relationship with the eternal God to the point where they become part of the process of bringing others into contact with Jesus Christ.

Attracting young people to attend an event where the Christian gospel is presented is the main feature of the delivery system. Over the past fifty years the primary models have included the club-to-rally approach of early Youth for Christ; the team-to-seeker event of Willow Creek's Student Impact; the club-to-camp approach of Young Life and later Youth for Christ; facility-based approaches such as locally sponsored coffee houses or gymnasiums ministries; and the youth group-to-evangelistic event of Sonlife Ministries. All of these delivery systems depend on adults to create them and depend on young people to invite their spiritually seeking friends.

Retaining and training is the opposite end of the programmatic axis. Rather than an event or a series of

Programmatic Axis

ATTRACT

RETAIN/TRAIN

events it is a long-term process whereby spiritual commitments are strengthened and leadership qualities are developed. From formal classes in which the Bible and spiritual disciplines are taught to small accountability groups, and from Christian service opportunities to support and acceptance of the entire community of believers, the retain/train process provides structure designed to nourish the adolescent in spiritual growth.

The more the student is involved in direct evangelism, the less formal structure is necessary for the retain/train process. Discipleship becomes a by-product of the evangelistic encounters. Students have to grow spiritually in order to survive.

The cycle of youth ministry is complete when a non-believing teenager has been contacted by a peer or adult, has been attracted to attend events where the Christian truth confronts the student and when that person is assimilated

Evangelism-based Ministry

ATTRACT

RETAIN/TRAIN

into a formal nurturing process. The end product will be young people who are actively involved in contacting spiritually sensitive peers in hopes of bringing them to Christ.

Adult roles

The dominant models of youth ministry current today were developed at a time when there was a Christian consensus both in the church and in society. Under such circumstances the old adage 'love 'em and feed 'em' may have been all that was necessary to do youth ministry. Students felt guilt. Moral standards were clear, even if exaggerated somewhat by over-protective parents and preachers. A common biblical foundation was understood. The greater problem existed in methodologies which were oblivious to human development and diverse learning styles.

As the twentieth century draws to a close the student is radically different from his counterpart of even twenty years ago. Today it is doubtful if a Christian consensus exists in either church or society. The authority of scripture in understanding truth, the moral accountability to the ten commandments in daily ethical decisions, the perspective of eternal life in dealing with human suffering and the existence of sin can no longer be assumed to be part of an adolescent's view of the world.

The role of the adult in working with youth today must maintain a balance which may not have been as necessary when families, schools and churches combined to form an integrated delivery system for discipleship. Some of the greatest models for maintaining an appropriate balance will, in all likelihood, come from places where secularism has forced the church and its youth to define itself apart from the culture rather than within it.

As in a delivery system, there are four components which define the role of the adult in discipleship (curiosity, need, commitment and truth). These roles are spread along two axes (prophet and shepherd). These roles are shown in the diagram below.

Adult Roles in Youth Ministry

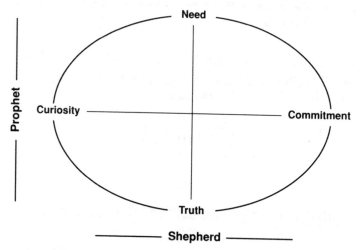

SHEPHERD AXIS

The shepherd axis (see diagram below) responds to two motivations of young people—curiosity and commitment. The shepherd's role is to capture the spiritual motivation created by the Holy Spirit and to transform it from curiosity about God to commitment to Jesus Christ. This corresponds to the relational axis of the delivery system.

Curiosity about religious activity remains socially based for most adolescents. They want to be with their friends, including adults whom they respect. If the friend of a curious person has an interest in knowing God, that fact becomes part of the relationship and has the potential of moving a person toward a commitment to Jesus Christ. There are other types of curiosity as well. An intellectual curiosity about God may cause a person to seek out a believer and to build a relationship around seeking answers. Moral curiosity may cause a young person who is concerned about justice and ethical issues to explore the views of a person who seems to have discovered consistency in daily life. Emotional curiosity may be evidenced in a person seeking unconditional love in this performance-based world.

Commitment is a giving or surrendering of all the student knows about himself or herself to all he or she has discovered about God in Jesus Christ. The value of this commitment is only as good as the integrity of the object of that commitment. The primary commitment is to the God of the Bible based on the redemptive work of Jesus Christ. Secondarily, a commitment needs to be made to the agencies

Shepherd Axis

CURIOSITY ⟷ COMMITMENT

which God ordained in society to bring about spiritual maturation—the family and the church.

There appears to be nothing the adult can do to hasten the movement from curiosity to commitment. Programmatic activity may help one person and confuse another. The shepherd is one who is sensitive to pacing and is willing to respond to the fluctuations of the adolescent temperament while keeping in view the developmental needs of the entire person.

PROPHET AXIS

The prophet axis (see diagram on page 116) focuses on two aspects of the human/eternal equation—felt needs and eternal truth. Though aspects of eternal truth must be grasped before a person can make a Christian commitment, the majority of one's lifetime will need to be committed to responding to the eternal truth discovered in the Bible. Some young people, however, find the truth claims of Christianity in an age of relativism to be the most attractive aspect of the prophetic voice. By contrast, most youth find truth most meaningful when it is applied to their felt needs. Consequently the following diagram includes two arrows to indicate the interactive nature of need and truth.

Felt needs in adolescents are so varied that it would be hard to list them all. Robert Havighurst may have best summarized these needs in his delineation of developmental tasks of adolescents. His list includes:

⊙ accepting one's physique and accepting a masculine or feminine role;

⊙ developing new relationships with age-mates of both sexes;

⊙ achieving emotional independence of parents and other adults;

Prophet Axis

NEED

TRUTH

⊙ achieving assurance of economic independence;

⊙ selecting and preparing for an occupation;

⊙ developing intellectual skills and concepts necessary for civic competence;

⊙ desiring and achieving socially responsible behaviour;

⊙ preparing for marriage and family life;

⊙ building conscious values in harmony with an adequate scientific world-picture.[2]

Most youth ministers today would translate this list into a series of questions such as: Who am I? Who can I trust? How can I be myself and still get along with my parents? How can I make the kind of living I want? How much and what kind of schooling do I need? How can I stay out of trouble? What are love and sex all about? Activities and experiences which deal with these kinds of questions enable the youthworker to engage students within their culture.

On the opposite end of the prophet axis is the presentation of biblical truth. It is this aspect of youth ministry which sets it apart from social work or child care. Christian truth provides a framework for understanding both the magnificence and depravity of human beings because of the greatness of the God who created them, allowed them to rebel and now offers to correct eternally their very nature. All of this is known, not on the basis of autonomous reason but as a result of God's written revelation.

Revealed truth is foreign to adolescents today. Teenagers in a post-modern world have no problem accepting Christianity as true but not as true. For them the truth of the ten commandments can live comfortably beside the truth of hedonistic playboy philosophy without conflict or apparent discrepancy. It is the responsibility of the youth minister/prophet to stake out a distinctive claim for revealed truth.

When the 'Delivery System in Youth Ministry' diagram is superimposed on the 'Adult Roles in Youth Ministry' diagram, a composite picture of the process of youth discipleship emerges (see diagram on page 118). At the same time it provides a framework in which the current youth ministry contributions can be understood, as well as a means to identify the emerging trends in the church's nurturing of young people.

Existing youth ministries

A closer look at the process of discipleship suggests four distinct emphases—bringing, converting, strengthening and sending. These correspond with the four quadrants of the diagram. As youthwork approaches the end of its second century and completes a third cycle of specialized ministry,

Process of Youth Discipleship

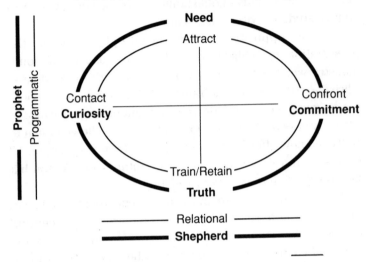

certain niches have been established in the youth ministry delivery system. While nearly every youth ministry agency operates in all four quadrants of the delivery system, each type of ministry has primary strengths in one part of the discipleship process.

When viewed as a whole, youth ministry could be described as having an effective impact, at least among the people who have the financial wherewithal to participate in the various delivery systems. Within the past ten years the leaders of a few of the major youth ministry agencies have begun to meet to pray and discuss their shared concerns. Even with this encouraging development, most of the players in the process of discipleship are more focused on what they are doing than on how a generation can best be reached for Jesus Christ.

BRINGING/CONVERTING

Those people who are the strongest at the bringing/converting part of the delivery system are parachurch clubs like Young Life, Youth for Christ (YFC), Fellowship of Christian Athletes and Student Venture. Coffee houses, drop-in centres, concerts by Christian musical artists and youth evangelists also play an important role in this part of youth ministry.

CONVERTING/STRENGTHENING

Perhaps the greatest weakness in the delivery system lies in the ability to translate converts into life-long followers of Jesus Christ. Many adolescents who stay will appear to be walking with Christ and growing stronger in their Christian faith as long as they have a continuity with those who were instrumental in bringing them into a commitment to Christ. But when the high school days are over and the support of Christian peers dissipates due to college and career commitments, the system tends to break down.

The Student Impact strategy of Willow Creek Community Church has attempted to address this problem by bringing the delivery system within the continuity of a local church. Though the people outside the Willow Creek Church view the discipleship system as working well, the leadership of Student Impact is currently in the process of making significant changes designed to increase their effectiveness in turning new converts into 'fully devoted followers of Jesus Christ'.

STRENGTHENING

When looking at all of the energy which is funneled into local church youth ministry, including Sunday School, youth groups and church-based clubs (Awana, Christian Service Brigade, Pioneer Clubs, Word of Life Clubs), and a variety of published materials designed to service those efforts, it is safe to suggest that the majority of youth ministry effort in the world is designed to strengthen adolescents in their Christian faith during a period of life when doubt is a natural product of human development.

Issue-generated movements (True Love Waits, See You at the Pole, Students Against Driving Drunk, Just Say No) are wonderful tools to help strengthen the values of Christian students. New Bible club movements (The Christian Club Campaign, Youth Alive Campus Ministry and Youth America Campus Clubs), as well as aspects of older club movements which had been influenced by the International Fellowship of Evangelical Students (Inter-School Christian Fellowship and Scripture Union), have as their focus the fortifying of believers for the work of ministry in their world.

Publishers of curricular materials as well as magazines aimed at Christian youth serve to strengthen young believers. All are vital parts of the holistic delivery system of youth ministry.

STRENGTHENING/SENDING

Some church youth groups which are lead by gifted youthworkers are able to move from merely strengthening youth to sending students out to do ministry. Agencies which train students to be part of the church's mission are especially important in this role. Some of these include Sonlife Missions and Evangelism Conference, Centre for Student Missions, Youth with a Mission, Teen Missions and World Servants.

Camp and conference ministries use the intensive time students are away from their normal setting to challenge and prepare youth to become part of the mission of the church. These efforts are especially effective when connected with parachurch agencies which can provide a strategy for bringing spiritually open students into confrontation with the Christian gospel.

The diagram on page 121 suggests a holistic picture of youth ministry at the end of the twentieth century. Though there are many other specific agencies, the groupings listed in the diagram encompass most aspects of the youth ministry delivery system.

Emerging youth ministries

There appears to be an explosion of innovation in youth ministry in the Western hemisphere. While the author has heard of similar entrepreneurial efforts in other parts of the world, documentation has been more difficult to obtain. Published reports, magazine articles as well as personal accounts of new ministry strategies would be helpful in gaining a more complete picture of youth ministry across the world.[3]

A sample of emerging youth ministries will provide a perspective on the breadth of efforts by God's people to reach the current generation of youth. It should be noted that not all of these innovations are new. In fact, some of the novelty comes from *who* or *where* a strategy is being employed.

Process in Existing Youth Ministries

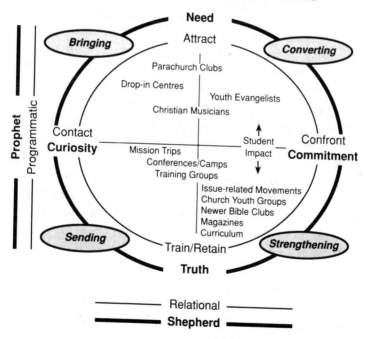

Disabled Teens—Melissa Manos is working with Young Life in Dallas, Texas. She has built relationships with developmentally disabled young people and works to bring them to camp.[4]

See You at the Pole—This movement began in Dallas-Fort Worth in 1989 with a small gathering of high school students. The idea was picked up by Texas Baptist youth leaders in 1990. That year the numbers reached 48,000 on 1,200 campuses in four states. There were an estimated 1.5 million in 1993 and as many as 2 million in 1994. The idea has gone international with reports from Singapore, Canada, the Philippines, Guatemala, Taiwan, Saipan, Russia, Austria, Albania, Romania and Belgium. In a press release, National Network of Youth Ministries reported that seventy denominations and Christian organizations participated in 1993. Over 35,000 students participated in Canada.[5]

Campus Christian Clubs—In 1994 over 9,000 student-led clubs flooded the campuses of the United States. Miami YFC reports evangelistic clubs on twenty-four of Dade County's twenty-six high schools.[6] The American Centre for Law and Justice, founded by Pat Robertson, estimates that 12,000 Bible clubs are operating in American public schools (this apparently goes beyond high schools); Student Venture is helping organize prayer groups that have 177,000 participants.[7]

Mentoring Moms—This ministry to teen mothers is a ministry of Young Life begun by Mary Sommerville in Visalia, California in 1991. The programme is expanding so rapidly that Cliff Anderson, Interim Director of the Institute for Youth Ministries, is working with Mary to form a network. On 25–28 August 1994, the Young Life camp, Woodleaf, hosted the second annual Mentoring Moms camp for Western states. Mary has written a book, *Mentoring Moms: A Handbook for Mentoring Teen Moms*.[8]

National Youth Crisis Hotline—1-800-HIT-HOME, a

ministry of Youth Development International (YDI), hears from 30,000 troubled teens per month. Bob Botsford has been YDI Director since 1990 but the work of YDI has been around for thirty-five years. Bob also serves as one of the pastors at Horizon Christian Fellowship in San Diego. The hotline connects callers with one of the 17,000 youth and social services nationwide. To get more information call 1-800-447-6263.[9]

Madison Urban Ministry—In 1989 Christ Presbyterian Church of Madison, Wisconsin made a long-term commitment to sixteen sixth-graders at a public school to mentor and tutor them, help them finish high school and then offer to help them with their college tuition. The effort was called Project Opportunity. From that effort, Monday night tutoring was initiated pairing thirty members of Christ Presbyterian Church with at-risk youth for one year. The programme has grown to be a city-wide, multi-church mentoring and tutoring effort known as Madison Urban Ministry. The effort, supported by Young Life, is interracial and inter-generational.[10]

Home Schooling—Home School Legal Defense Association and National Centre for Home Education estimate that 500,000 families home schooled their children in 1990. The US Department of Education placed the number in 1991 between 250,000 and 350,000. Typical income of a home schooling family ranges between $25,000 and $35,000 with both parents having attended college.[11]

Youth For Christ Ministry Models—In 1991, YFC published 'A nationwide selection of effective ministry events, programmes and outreach ideas for the contemporary youthworker.' In it were grouped seven clusters of models:

⊙ One-on-one—Tutoring programme, Teen Pregnancy House, Daytime Shelter, After-school Hobby Workshop, Outreach to Pregnant Teens and Vocational Interest Programmes.

⊙ Small Group—Small Group Outreach, Specialized Small Groups, Divorce Groups, Referral Based Small Groups, Unwed Mothers Outreach and Vacation Bible Schools.

⊙ Large Group—High School Breakfast Club, Abstinence Training, Weekly Group Meetings, After-school Clubs, School Services, Neighborhood Outreach, Gang Impact Ministry, Friday Night Alternative and Drop-in Centre.

⊙ Rally—Kick-off Event, Youth Rally, Indoor Sports Competition and Friday Night After the Game.

⊙ Mobilizing Models—Church Partnerships, Housing Projects/Church Partnerships, Church Liaisons, Student Leadership and Student Leaders Training.

⊙ Sports/Outdoor Recreation—Three-on-Three Basketball Tournament, Flag Football, National Youth Project Using Mini-Bikes, Bicycling Club, Overnight Camping, Water Ski School, Three-on-Three Basketball League and Karate Club.

⊙ Follow-Up—Follow-up as a Ministry Division, Institution Ministry Follow-up Program.[12]

SportsLife—Todd James of Greater Europe Mission has begun a ministry which is seeking to use Christian coaches not only to increase athletic skills but also to gain a hearing for the gospel. SportsLife is based in Ireland but is seeking to expand throughout Europe.[13]

Skateboard evangelism—Eddie Elguera travels across the United States putting on demonstrations and then sharing the gospel in conjunction with local churches and evangelistic efforts. The 1979 and 1980 world champion continues to attract admirers from a subculture which can appreciate the skill and conviction of a man who can do a 720-degree Elgurial—spinning two times in the air and landing backwards on his skateboard.[14]

Urban Youth Ministry—'Youth ministry is moving to the city,' concludes Ed Robinson of Nazarene Theological Seminary. 'Developing youth ministers for the future will necessitate an awareness of the international flavor of the world in general and the American city in particular.'

After visiting five metropolitan settings, Robinson identified four basic models of urban youth ministries—local church-based (traditional ethnic congregation such as Beulah Community Church of the Nazarene, Brooklyn, New York [David Solomon]; multicultural community congregation such as Lawndale Community Church, Chicago, Illinois [Wayne Gordon]; transitioning congregation such as Immanuel Presbyterian Church, Los Angeles, California [Mitch Moore]; ministry-sponsoring congregations such as Bresee Youth Services/First Church of the Nazarene, Los Angeles, California [Jeff Carr]); Community Agencies (parachurch such as Focus on Relationships, San Francisco, California [Mike DeTiranto]; emerging church such as Bruce Wall Ministries, Boston, Massachusetts [Bruce Wall]); National Parachurch (Young Life of Boston, Boston, Massachusetts [Chris Troy]); Individual Entrepreneurs such as The Iron Pit/The Righteous Few, Oakland, California [Gary Shields]).[15]

Hampton Youth Service Centre—Elmon Hampton, a 60-year-old Baptist deacon, runs a youth centre in the basement and backyard of his home on West Washington Boulevard in Chicago. Funded primarily by Hampton and staffed by six people (friends, neighbours and relatives), the centre opens to seventy or so children each day who come to participate in tutoring, Bible studies, basketball, using playground equipment, as well as playing video games. On weekends as many as twenty-five college students converge on the Youth Service Centre to assist in the effort to minister to young people on the west side of Chicago.[16]

These innovations are but a recent sampling of youth ministry efforts. The question which must be asked, however, is not *What is happening?* but *How does a youth minister make sense of what is happening?* To put it another way, *What are the emerging patterns of youth ministry?*

Emerging patterns of youth ministry

Ten observations can be made about emerging youth ministries and for better or worse these form the patterns of Christian youth ministry at the end of the twentieth century. Most of these patterns will make sense when placed within the context of the diagram used earlier.

⊙ Emerging youth ministries are relational. They are most effective in the bringing and converting aspects of the delivery system. These are primarily shepherding functions which respond to perceived needs in young people. Melissa Manos' work with disabled youth begins with building a relationship. Todd James' work with Irish athletes begins with a common interest and time spent together building a relationship. In The Iron Pit, Gary Shields builds relationships with African-American young people by training them to 'pump iron' (lift weights).

⊙ Emerging youth ministries are grassroots movements. Initial success brings local support and only later does encouragement come from established youth ministry agencies, churches and publishers. Strategic leadership in youth ministry will be needed to discover and support such innovations as they appear. Youth for Christ promoted ministry strategies based on local initiatives such as tutoring programmes, abstinence training, drop-in centres and gang impact ministries.

⊙ Emerging youth ministries need connectedness. Seldom are they effective in all four quadrants of the youth ministry delivery system (bringing, converting, strengthening and sending). They need to be connected with and accountable to ministries which are strong in the other areas of ministry. Eddie Elguera's skateboard ministry is connected with local evangelistic outreaches; Bresee Youth Services in Los Angeles are associated with First Church of the Nazarene; Elmon Hampton was involved in ministry in a Baptist church for thirty years before opening the Hampton Youth Service Centre and finds that connectedness essential for the functioning of the Centre.

⊙ Emerging youth ministries are niche oriented. They are focused on one idea or one social grouping. See You at the Pole draws people from diverse backgrounds to public prayer. Mentoring Moms finds ways to help unwed mothers who are teenagers. National Youth Crisis Hotline targets troubled teens. True Love Waits promotes sexual purity. None of these are seeking to reach and hold the entire spectrum of young people in one unified strategy.

⊙ Emerging youth ministries are inter-generational. Though student ownership and leadership are essential, adults are the initiators of new youth ministries. The more

Emerging Youth Ministries

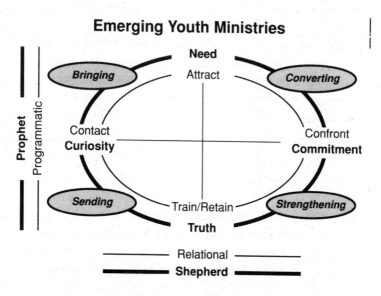

generations engage, the greater is the possibility of diversity in the young people being reached. None of the innovations cited above were initiated by adolescents.

⊙ Emerging youth ministries are poorly funded. Many are not funded at all. Instead new movements tend to be passion-driven, sacrifice-fed and results-focused. Though there is a limit to how long these 'lean and mean' movements can sustain themselves, the more effective ministries will survive until additional provision is supplied by God's people. Hampton Youth Service Centre is funded primarily by Hampton himself. Youth America Campus Clubs are based upon student initiatives and lay sponsors. The home schooling movement is the sole responsibility of parents.

⊙ Emerging youth ministries are theologically vulnerable. They have a better understanding of human nature than attributes of God. Some have become so earthly-minded that they are of little heavenly use. Few have recognized the essential core of beliefs which identify them with historic Christianity. Others fail to recognize that co-belligerency against sin does not bond them in a covenant relationship. No doctrinal standard is required to 'see you at the pole'. Crisis hotlines have a great enough problem keeping up with 30,000 calls each month without requiring a thorough integration of a biblical worldview and counselling skills.

⊙ Emerging youth ministries are the expressions of the church in transition. Churches which have continuity of ministry from generation to generation seldom have a need for innovative youth ministries. But when the culture around the church changes as rapidly as the youth culture of the 1990s has done, churches begin wondering if their own mission is clear and at the same time look for outside help for their youth. Madison Urban Ministry came out of churches in transitional communities. Church partnerships with Youth for Christ or Young Life usually reflect church leaders who no longer find themselves able to satisfy the concerns of anxious parents in their midst.

⊙ Emerging youth ministries clarify values. Most are a means of passing Christian values from one generation to the next. If the family or church have strayed from the values discovered in the Bible, new ministries emerge to bring correctives to the situation. Home schooling and Hampton Youth Services Centre attempt to assist families to become examples of academic excellence and moral integrity.

⊙ Emerging youth ministries should think of themselves as church-planting strategies. The idea of helping students through their adolescent years and then turning them over to church leaders with whom they have little if any relationship has not been highly successful in the past, and there is little reason to suspect a greater degree of success in the future. Once youth leaders have earned the right to be trusted by adolescents, that relationship should be maintained, wherever possible, for a lifetime. In this age of mobility, such an expectation might be impossible but at least the possibility of long-term relationships in the context of a witnessing community should be attempted.

Conclusion

Perhaps the key to innovations in youth ministry is people like Tony, the African-American youthworker from Indianapolis, paired with people who can see the big picture. The combination of 'street smarts' in the younger person and perspective gained over years of studying youth ministry could provide that ministry with a much needed infusion of spiritual power.

NOTES

1. Translated: 'They are ideas dreamed up by some middle-class Anglo-American who lives in an affluent suburb in order to keep bored rich kids happy.'.

2. Robert James Havighurst, *Human Development and Education*, New York: David McKay Co., 1953, pp. 111–58.

3. Documentation of youth ministry innovations should be sent to Mark H. Senter III, at Trinity Evangelical Divinity School, 2065 Half Day Road, Deerfield, IL 60015, United States.

4. *Inside Young Life*, November 1994, Volume 1, No. 8, p. 1.

5. *The Network News*, Winter 1994, Volume 12, No. 3, p. 3 'Media Alert', press release from Doug Clark NNYM, September 14, 1994.

6. '1994 Forum Report', National Network of Youth Ministries, pp. 1, 3.

7. 'Prayer already in U.S. schools', *Chicago Tribune*, November 24, 1994; section 1, p. 34. Some of the newer agencies promoting campus clubs include: The Christian Club Campaign, PO Box 552, Little Rock, AR 72203, (501) 376-4791 ext. 5132; Youth Alive Campus Ministry, 1445 Boonville Ave, Springfield, MO 65802, (800) 545-2766; Youth America Campus Clubs, PO Box 20,000, Oklahoma City, OK 73156, (405) 947-2000 (Ray Hollis); *The Network News*, Spring 1994, Volume 12, No. 1, p. 5.

The more established high school campus ministries include: Rod Handley, Fellowship of Christian Athletes, 8701 Leeds Rd, Kansas City, MO 64129, 816-921-0909, 800-289-0909; Chuck Klein, Student Venture, 17150 Via del Campo, Suite 200, San Diego, CA 92127-9969, 619-487-2717, 619-487-8915 (FAX); Mike Calhoun, Word of Life Clubs, Schroon Lake, NY 12870; Roger Cross, Youth for Christ United States, Denver, Box 228822, Denver, CO 80222, 303-843-9000; Denny Rydberg, Young Life, Box 520, Colorado Springs, CO 80901, 719-473-4262.

8. Contact Mary Sommerville, Mentoring Moms, 1819 E. Seeger Ave, Visalia, CA 93292; phone 209-734-7232. *Inside Young Life*, November 1994, Volume 1, No. 6, p. 2.

9. *The Network News*, Fall 1994, Volume 12, No. 2, p. 4.

10. Dale Buss, 'Close Encounters Across Cultures', *Christianity Today*, December 12, 1994, pp. 15–16.

11. 'Home Schooling Alternative Grows', *Youthworker Update*, December 1994, pp. 5–6.

12. *Ministry Models Manual*, [Denver]: Youth for Christ/United States, 1991

13. Personal correspondence from Todd James, SportsLife, 4 College Grove, Castleknock, Dublin 15, Ireland; tel. 217916.

14. Thomas S. Giles, 'Eddie the Cat Comes Back', *Christianity Today*, September 14, 1992, pp. 16–17.

15. Ed Robinson, 'A Survey of Urban Youth Ministry Models: Preliminary Findings', unpublished paper presented at NAPCE Conference, October, 1992.

16. George Papajohn and Byron P. White, 'Community Warriors', *Chicago Tribune*, December 20, 1994, Section 1, pp. 1, 16.

Notes

Notes

Notes

Notes

Notes

Notes

Notes

Notes

Notes

Notes

Notes

Notes

Notes